Computing Excellence :

Empowering Future Engineers

Prof.Sir.Bashiru Aremu
Prof.Dr.K .Mahammad Rafi
Dr.Mir.Iqbal Faheem
Dr. Mohd Minhajuddin Aquil

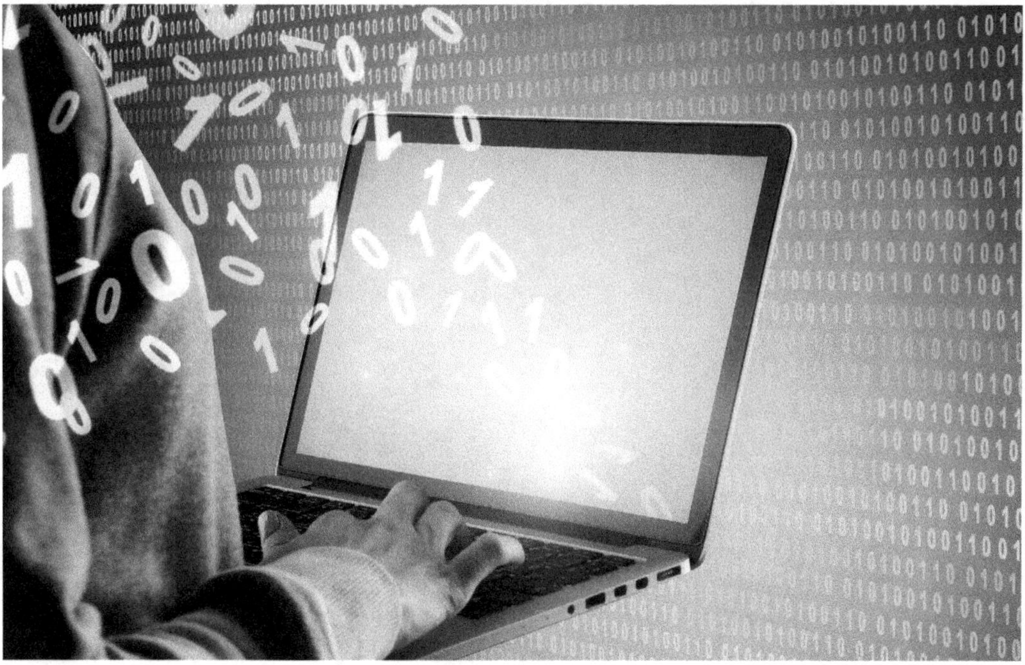

Doctorate Int'l Publications
Dept. of Research & Publications
eSkillGrow Virtual University LLC USA
CoE @India, Japan, Germany, Poland, Malaysia

Prof.Sir.Bashiru Aremu
Prof.Dr.K .Mahammad Rafi
Dr.Mir.Iqbal Faheem
Dr. Mohd Minhajuddin Aquil

Doctorate Publications

Imprint

any brand names and product names mentioned in this book are subject to trademark, brand or patent protection and are trademarks or registered trademarks of their respective holders. the use of brand names, product names, common names, trade names, product descriptions etc. even without a particular marking in this work is in no way to be construed to mean that such names may be regarded as unrestricted in respect of trademark and brand protection legislation and could thus be used by anyone.

Cover Image: www.canva.com

publisher:
Doctorate publications
is an International Publishing house
under Department of Research & Publications
@ eSkilllGrow Virtual University LLCs(regd as per usa govt int'l laws)

INDIA:
  1.   4&5, arpita enclave, karmanghat, hyderabad, telangana

USA :

  1.   International Regd agent office at Delaware and California, USA
16192.coastal highway city of Lewes.

  2.   Administrative Office of Registered agents inc.   90 state street, ste 700 office 40, albany 12207 , county: albany, New York city, USA

  3.   e-101 kitchawan rd, yorktown heights, ny 10598, USA

GERMANY:
  1.   34/09-a, geschwister-scholl-straße 7, d-39307 genthin, germany

JAPAN:
  4.   a-19-21, ihonbashihakozakichō, chūō-ku, tōkyō-to-103-0015, japan.

POLAND:
  5.   b-2/45, ul. a. kręglewskiego 11, 61-248-2 poznań, poland

Computing Excellence:

Empowering Future Engineers

Doctorate Publications

CONTENTS

MODULE 1

CHAPTER 1 A BEGINNER'S GUIDE

INTRODUCTION TO COMPUTERS

On a computer, any programming language is implemented. Since their creation to the current day, all computers (regardless of their size and shape) have performed the following 5 fundamental activities. It transforms the unprocessed input data into information that the users may use.

☐ **Inputting**: It entails entering information and commands into the computer system.

☐ **Storing**: The information and instructions are saved for use in initial or subsequent processing as needed.

☐ **Processing**: To transform the recorded data into useable information, arithmetic or logical operations must be applied to it.

☐ **Outputting**: It is the procedure for creating output data for the customer.

☐ **Controlling**: To be successful, the aforementioned actions need to be carried out in a specific order.

Based on these 5 operations, we can sketch the block diagram of a computer.

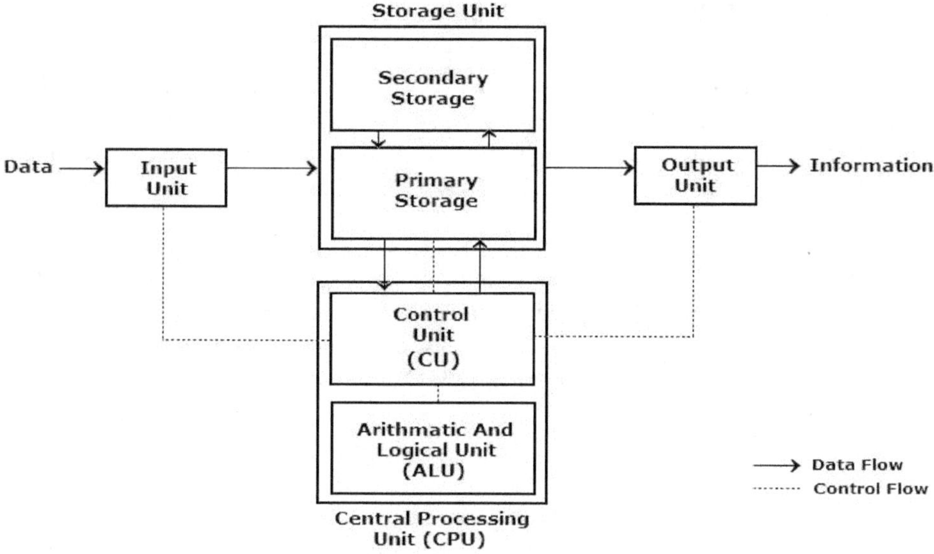

Fig 1: Block Diagram of a Computer

☐ **Input Unit:** Before any computation can take place, we must first enter the necessary data and instructions into the computer system. The input devices complete this duty for us. (Examples include a keyboard, mouse, scanner, digital camera, etc.). This gadget is in charge of connecting the system to the outside world. The accepted data is presented in a human understandable format. It is transformed into a computer-readable format by the input device.

☐ **Storage Unit:** The computer has to store the data and instructions that are entered. Similar to the intermediate results, the final results must also be stored before being sent to the output unit. The storage unit offers a fix for each of these problems. The starting data, the intermediate result, and the final result are all designed to be saved in this storage unit. Primary storage and Secondary storage are both included in this storage unit.

Primary Storage: When the computer is turned on, the data is kept in the primary storage, also known as the main memory. The information kept in primary storage is volatile in nature and disappears as soon as the machine is turned off or restarted. Furthermore, because it is made up of pricey semiconductor devices, primary storage often has a low storage capacity.

Secondary Storage: The primary memory's storage constraints and volatile nature are handled by the secondary storage, also known as the auxiliary storage. Even after the system is turned off, information can still be retained. Basically, it's utilised to store programme instructions and data that the computer needs to process later but isn't working on right now.

☐ **Central Processing Unit:** The Control Unit and the Arithmetic Logic Unit are collectively referred to as the Central Processing Unit (CPU). The CPU is the computer's mental centre. Like in humans, the brain itself makes the key decisions, and other bodily parts carry out the brain's instructions. The CPU performs all of the significant calculations and comparisons in a computer system similarly. The CPU is in charge of turning on and controlling the operation of other computer system components.

Arithmetic Logic Unit: Here, the instructions (arithmetic or logical operations) are really put to use. The primary storage's data and instructions are sent as and when they are needed. The primary store is not used for processing. ALU generates intermediate results, which are momentarily sent back to the primary store until later required. As a result, data may transit between the primary store and the ALU and back again numerous times before the processing is finished.

Control Unit: Although it doesn't really process any data, this unit manages how the entire computer functions. It is in charge of transferring information and commands between the computer's many components. It oversees and plans the operation of every system component.

Input/Output devices are also communicated with in order to transfer data or results from the storage units.

☐ **Output Unit:** An output unit's function is the exact opposite of that of an input unit. It accepts computer-generated results in coded form. It transforms these coded results into readable human form. Finally, it uses output devices (such as monitors, printers, projectors, etc.) to show the converted results to the outside world.

Consequently, when we refer to a computer, we really imply two things:

☐ **Hardware-** The entire physical operation of the computer is carried out by this hardware.

☐ **Software-** The hardware is told what to do and how to do it by this software. The computer system is made up of both the hardware and the software. System software and application software are further categories for this software.

System Software- A group of programmes known as system software are in charge of managing computer resources, operating the computer, and controlling other computer system processes. They serve as a bridge between the computer's hardware and application software. Operating system, for instance.

Application Software- Application software is a group of programmes created to help users with a specific issue. It enables the end user to perform tasks other than just using the gear. For instance, a web browser or gaming software.

CHAPTER 2

INTRODUCTION TO PROGRAMMING

Programming, often known as coding, is the process of writing a series of instructions in a language that is understandable by a computer system. Computer languages are also referred to as programming languages. A programme is a collection of instructions created by a computer to carry out a certain activity. Software refers to a collection of extensive programmes. One needs to be knowledgeable about a programming language to create software.

It's necessary to understand the many kinds of languages used by computers before tackling any programming languages. Let's first understand what the programmers' fundamental needs were and what challenges they encountered when writing programmes in that language.

COMPUTER LANGUAGES

A means of communication is language. People typically communicate with one another through language. A language is used to communicate with computers in a similar manner.

Both the user and the machine can understand this language. Every computer language is constrained by the syntax rules of that language, just as every language, including Hindi and English, has its own set of grammatical rules. This syntax controls all communications between the user and the computer system.

Computer languages are broadly classified as:

☐ **Low Level Language**: Low level refers to the notion that it is more similar to a language that a computer can understand.

These are the low level languages:

o **Machine Language**: This is the language that the computer can understand directly (in the form of binary digits, which are made up of 0s and 1s). It is reliant on machines. It's challenging to learn, and writing programmes is even harder.

o **Assembly Language**: In order to aid in learning, symbolic codes (referred to as mnemonics) are used in place of the machine codes, which are made up of 0s and 1s. It is the initial stage in improving the structure of programming. Programming in assembly language is less complicated and time-consuming than programming in machine language, and it is also simpler to find and fix faults in assembly language programmes than in machine language programmes. Additionally, it is machine-reliant. The computer that will run the programme must be understood by programmers.

☐ **High Level Language:** Since low level language is machine dependant, it necessitates substantial hardware understanding. High level language, which uses everyday English that is simple to comprehend to address any problem, has evolved to get around this limitation. Programming becomes incredibly straightforward and easy because to high level languages, which are independent of computers. The following list of high level languages includes:

- BASIC (Beginners All Purpose Symbolic Instruction Code): This general-purpose language is popular and simple to learn. formerly primarily found in microcomputers.
- Common Business Oriented Language (COBOL) is a standardised language used in business applications.
- FORTRAN (Formula Translation): Designed to address issues in mathematics and science. of the most widely used languages in the scientific community.
- C: A structured programming language used for a variety of tasks, including creating games and doing research.
- C++: A well-known, general-purpose object-oriented programming language.

PROGRAMMING LANGUAGE TRANSLATORS

As you are aware, while assembly language is machine dependent and high level language is machine independent, the mnemonics used to represent instructions in assembly language are not directly readable by machines. Programming language instructors are thus utilised to make the computer understand the instructions provided by both languages. They convert the programmers' instructions into a format that the computer can understand and carry out. The different tools that can be used to accomplish this goal are flowing:

☐ **Compiler**: Compiler refers to the software that reads a programme written in high level language and converts it into a machine language equivalent. The source programme is the one created by the programmer in high-level language, while the object programme is the one produced by the compiler following translation.

☐ **Interpreter**: Additionally, it carries out commands written in high-level languages. Although compliers and interpreters share the same objective, which is to translate high level language into binary instructions, they operate in distinct ways. The interpreter takes one statement, translates it, executes it, and then takes the next statement. The compiler transforms the complete source code into a machine-level programme.

☐ **Assembler**: Assemblers are pieces of software that read assembly language programmes and convert them into their machine language equivalents.

☐ **Linker**: A computer programme known as a linker or link editor merges one or more object files produced by a compiler into a single executable file, library file, or additional object file.

CHAPTER 3

Brief History of C

☐ Dennis Ritchie created the structure-oriented programming language known as C at Bell Laboratories in 1972.

☐ Features of the "B" (Basic Combined computer Language, or BCPL) computer language were adapted into the "C" programming language.

☐ The UNIX operating system was implemented using the C programming language.

☐ Dennis Ritchie and Brian Kernighan published the first edition of "The C Programming Language" in 1978; this book is also referred to as K&R C.

☐ A group to develop a current, thorough description of C was established in 1983 by the American National Standards Institute (ANSI). The resulting definition, known as the "ANSI C" standard, was finished in late 1988.

☐ This new language was given the name "C" since it borrowed many concepts and tenets from the prior language B.

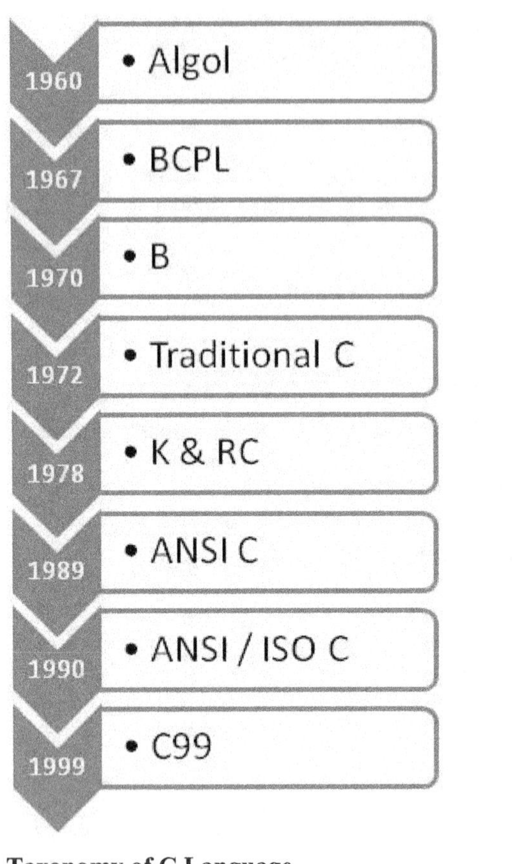

Taxonomy of C Language

WHY IS C POPULAR

☐ It is dependable, clear, and straightforward to use.

☐ Small and block-based, C is a programming language.

☐ Because C is a portable language, programmes created in it can run with little to no modification on several platforms.

☐ One of the most comprehensive collections of operators, including those for calculations and data comparisons, is found in C.

☐ Although the programmer has more latitude when it comes to data storage, the languages do not examine the programmer's data types for accuracy.

WHY TO STUDY C

☐ Early in the 1980s, C was already the language of choice for Unix systems on minicomputers. Since then, it has migrated to mainframes and personal computers (microcomputers).

☐ C is frequently used by software companies to create word processing applications, spreadsheets, compilers, and other products.

☐ Particularly when it comes to writing operating systems, C is a very flexible language.

☐ C contains fifteen levels of precedence, compared to the four or five found in most other languages.

CHARECTERESTICS OF A C PROGRAM

☐ Middle level language

High Level	Middle Level	Low Level
High level languages provide almost everything that the programmer might need to do as already built into the language	Middle level languages don't provide all the built-in functions found in high level languages, but provides all building blocks that we need to produce the result we want	Low level languages provides nothing other than access to the machines basic instruction set
Examples: Java, Python	C, C++	Assembler

☐ Small size - has only 32 keywords

☐ The C library can be expanded by the end user by using function calls often.

☐ supports loose typing, allowing for the treatment of a character as an integer and vice versa.

☐ Structured language

Structure oriented	Object oriented	Non structure
In this type of language, large programs are divided into small programs called functions	In this type of language, programs are divided into objects	There is no specific structure for programming this language
Prime focus is on functions and procedures that operate on the data	Prime focus is in the data that is being operated and not on the functions or procedures	N/A
Data moves freely around the systems from one function to another	Data is hidden and cannot be accessed by external functions	N/A
Program structure follows "Top Down Approach"	Program structure follows "Bottom UP Approach"	N/A
Examples: C, Pascal, ALGOL and Modula-2	C++, JAVA and C# (C sharp)	BASIC, COBOL, FORTRAN

☐ Low level (Bit Wise) programming readily available

☐ Pointer implementation - extensive use of pointers for memory, array, structures and functions.

☐ It has high-level constructs.

☐ It can handle low-level activities.

☐ It produces efficient programs.

☐ It can be compiled on a variety of computers.

USES

System applications, which make up the majority of operating systems like Windows, UNIX, and Linux, are developed using the C programming language. Here are some instances of C in use:

☐ Database systems

☐ Graphics packages

☐ Word processors

☐ Spreadsheets

☐ Operating system development

☐ Compilers and Assemblers

☐ Network drivers

☐ Interpreters

STRUCTURE OF A C PROGRAM

A C programmer must adhere to a protocol (set of rules) known as the C program's structure when writing a C programme. The image below depicts the general fundamental structure of a C programme.

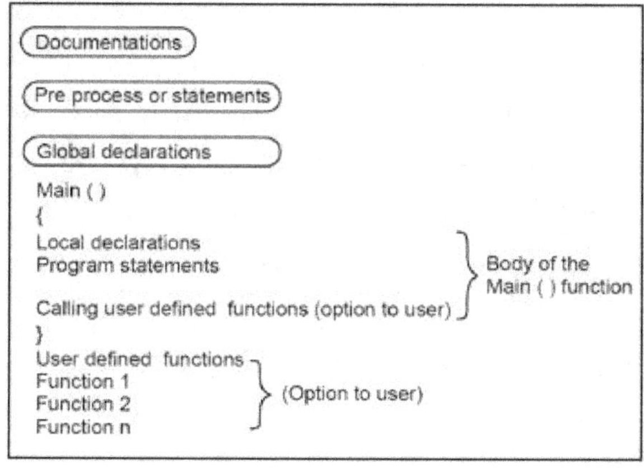

Based on this structure, we can sketch a C program.

Example:

```c
/* This program accepts a number & displays it to the user*/
#include <stdio.h>
void main(void)
{ int number;
printf( "Please enter a number: " );
scanf( "%d", &number );
printf( "You entered %d", number );
return 0;}
```

Stepwise explanation:

#include

☐ The preprocessor is the component of the compiler that actually extracts your programme from the source file.

☐ #include <stdio.h>

☐ A pre-processor directive is #include. It is a directive to the compiler to cause it to perform a task rather than actually being a component of our programme. In this situation, the system file stdio.h, it instructs the C compiler to include the contents of the file.

☐ Because the filename is encased in > characters, the compiler understands that it is a system file and must be located in a certain location.

<stdio.h>

☐ The standard library definition file for all STanDard Input and Output functions is called stdio.h.

☐ The file with the functions we want to utilise specified is called stdio.h, and your programme will almost definitely want to send information to the screen and read data from the keyboard.

☐ We want to use a function called printf. The linker will later tie in the actual printf code.

☐ An include file is identified by the language extension ".h" in the filename.

void

☐ This essentially means that nothing is being said. In this instance, it alludes to the function whose name is shown after.

☐ Void informs the C compiler that an entity is meaningless and does not cause an error.

main

☐ The program's sole function in this example is designated as main.

☐ Typically, a C programme consists of several different functions. The programmer gives each of these names, and when the software runs, they are all used to refer to one another.

☐ Since C views the term main as a special case, it will execute this function first, starting the programme at main.

(void)

☐ This is a pair of brackets enclosing the keyword void.

☐ It tells the compiler that the function main has no parameters.

☐ A parameter to a function gives the function something to work on.

{ (Brace)

☐ A brace (or curly bracket) is what this is. As the name suggests, braces are sold in pairs; there must be a close brace for every open brace.

☐ Programme components can be grouped together using braces, which are sometimes known as blocks.

☐ The declaration of a variable that will be utilised within a block may be followed by a series of programme statements.

☐ In this instance, the function main's operational components are enclosed by the braces.

; (semicolon)

☐ The list of variable names and that declaration statement are both concluded with a semicolon.

☐ C programmes use semicolons (";") to separate each statement.

☐ Actually, the character ";" is crucial. It communicates to the compiler the end of a particular statement.

☐ A compiler error will be generated if one of these characters is not present where it is expected to be scanf.

☐ The functions for printing and reading are built into various computer languages.

☐ Instead, they are defined as standard functions in C, which are a component of the language specification but not the language itself.

☐ There are several functions in the standard input/output library for transferring formatted data; the two we'll use are scanf (scan formatted) and printf (print formatted).

printf

☐ The printf function is the opposite of scanf.

☐ It projects text and values onto the screen using data from the programme.

☐ Similar to scanf, it is a feature of all versions of C and is explained in the system file stdio.h.

☐ The format string, which includes text, value descriptions, and formatting instructions, is the first parameter to a printf.

FILES USED IN A C PROGRAM

☐ **Source File-** The program's source code is located in this file. Any file created in C has the.c file extension. The main function and maybe other functions are defined in the file's C source code.

☐ **Header File-** A header file is a file with the extension.h that includes C function declarations and macro definitions and is intended to be shared by many source files.

☐ **Object File-** An object file is a file with the extension.o that contains object code, which is relocatable format computer code that is typically not directly executable. Object files are created by an assembler, compiler, or other language translator and sent through a linker, which commonly assembles the object files into an executable or library.

☐ **Executable File-** The linker creates the binary executable file. The linker joins the different object files to create an executable binary file.

COMPLIATION & EXECUTION OF A C PROGRAM

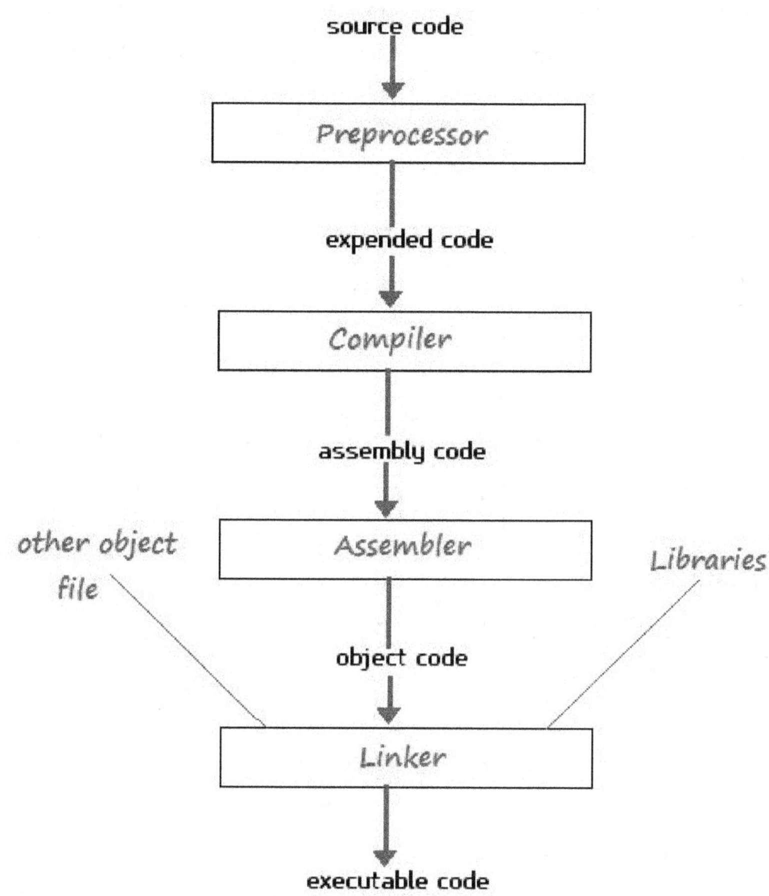

CHAPTER 4 ELEMENTS OF C

There are fundamental components and grammatical principles in every language. Before beginning to programme, we should be familiar with the fundamental building blocks of the language.

Character Set

Speaking the computer's language is necessary for communicating with it. Many different characters can communicate in C.

Character set in C consists of.

Types	Character Set
Lower case	a-z
Upper case	A-Z
Digits	0-9
Special Character	!@#$%^&*
White space	Tab or new lines or space

Keywords

The terms that have previously been defined for the C compiler are known as keywords. Because doing so would attempt to give the term a new meaning, which the computer does not permit, the keywords cannot be utilised as variable names.

In C, there are only 32 possible keywords. For your quick reference, a list of these terms is provided in the image below.

auto	do	goto	signed	unsigned
break	double	if	sizeof	void
case	else	int	static	volatile
char	enum	long	struct	while
const	extern	register	switch	
continue	float	return	typeodef	
default	for	short	union	

Identifier

An identifier in the computer language C is a string of alphanumeric characters, where the first character is either an alphabetic letter or an underline and the remaining characters can be any letter of the alphabet, any digit, or the underline.

When naming identifiers, two requirements must be followed.

1. Alphabetic characters have a case that matters. There is a difference between using "INDEX" and "index" and between using "Index" and "INDEX" for variables. All three make reference to various variables.

2. According to the definition of C, a maximum of 32 significant characters may be used; most compilers will treat them as such. The compiler will not utilise any more than 32 if they are present.

Data Type

Data types in the C programming language refer to a range of permitted values and the operations that can be carried out on those values. The type of a variable dictates how much storage space it takes up and how the stored bit pattern is interpreted. In C, there are four basic data types: char, int, float, and double. Any single letter can be stored in char; any integer value can be stored in int; any single precision floating point number can be stored in float; and any double precision floating point number can be stored in double. To create more types, we can combine these fundamental kinds with two qualifiers.

There are 2 types of qualifiers-

Sign qualifier- signed & unsigned

Size qualifier- short & long

The data types in C can be classified as follows:

Type	Storage size	Value range
char		-128 to 127
unsigned char	1 byte	0 to 255
int	2 or 4 bytes	-32,768 to 32,767 or -2,147,483,648to 2,147,483,647
unsigned int	2 or 4 bytes	0 to 65,535 or 0 to 4,294,967,295
Short	2 bytes	-32,768 to 32,767
unsigned short	2 bytes	0 to 65,535
long	4 bytes	-2,147,483,648 to 2,147,483,647
unsigned long	4 bytes	0 to 4,294,967,295

Type	Storage size	Value range	Precision
float	4 bytes	1.2E-38 to 3.4E+38	6 decimal places
double	8 bytes	2.3E-308 to 1.7E+308	15 decimal places
long double	10 bytes	3.4E-4932 to 1.1E+4932	19 decimal places

Constants

A variable is an entity that might vary, as opposed to a constant, which remains constant.

C constants can be divided into two major categories:

☐	Primary Constants

☐   Secondary Constants

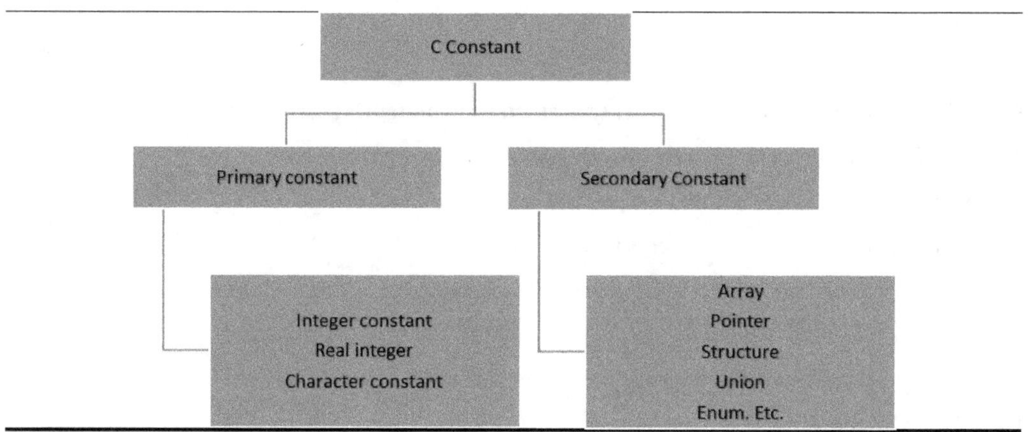

Here, we merely pay attention to the main constant. Certain guidelines have been established for the construction of these various types of constants.

Rules for Constructing Integer Constants:

An integer constant must have at least one digit.

a)   It must not have a decimal point.

b)   It can be either positive or negative.

c)   If no sign precedes an integer constant it is assumed to be positive.

d)   No commas or blanks are allowed within an integer constant.

e)   The allowable range for integer constants is -32768to 32767.

Ex.: 426, +782,-8000, -7605

Rules for Constructing Real Constants:

Floating Point constants are frequently used to refer to real constants. There are two ways to express real constants: in fractional form and in exponential form.

Rules for constructing real constants expressed in fractional form:

a)   A real constant must have at least one digit.

b)   It must have a decimal point.

c)   It could be either positive or negative.

d)   Default sign is positive.

e)   No commas or blanks are allowed within a real constant.

Ex. +325.34, 426.0, -32.76, -48.5792

Rules for constructing real constants expressed in exponential form:

a) There should be an e between the mantissa and the exponential parts.

b) A positive or negative sign may be present in the mantissa portion.

c) Mantissa part's default indication is positive.

d) A positive or negative integer must make up at least one of the exponent's digits. Sign is positive by default.

e) Real constants have an exponential expression that ranges from -3.4e38 to 3.4e38.

Ex. +3.2e-5, 4.1e8, -0.2e+3, -3.2e-5

Rules for Constructing Character Constants:

a) A single alphabet, one digit, or one unique special symbol wrapped in a single pair of inverted commas is referred to as a character constant.

b) A character constant can have a maximum length of one character.

Ex.: 'M', '6', '+'

CHAPTER 5 VARIABLES

Values are stored in names called variables. It can accept several values, but only one at a time. Each variable has a data type associated with it, which determines the possible values for the variable. Simply declare (or create) a new variable whenever you determine your programme requires one, and C will make sure you have access to it. All C variables are declared at the beginning of the relevant code blocks. You must tell C the name and data type of the variable when declaring it.

Syntax - datatype variablename;

Eg:

int page_no;

char grade;

float salary;

long y;

Declaring Variables:

There are two places where you can declare a variable:

☐ Immediately following a block of code's opening brace (often at the top of a function)

☐ Before a function name (for instance, before main() in the programme) Take a look at a few examples:

Imagine having to remember someone's first, middle, and last initials. The three initials should be stored in three character variables since an initial is obviously a character. You might accomplish that in C by using the following sentence:

1. main()

{

char first, middle, last;

// Rest of program follows

}

2. main()

{

char first;

char middle;

char last;

// Rest of program follows

}

Initialization of Variables

A variable holds undefined value, often known as garbage value, when it is declared. The variables can optionally be given an initial value during the declaration process. Initialization of the variable is what this is known as.

Eg-

int pageno=10;

char grade='A';

float salary= 20000.50;

Expressions

A mix of operators, operands, variables, and function calls make up an expression. A mathematical, logical, or relational expression are all possible. Here are a few phrases:

a+b - arithmetic operation

a>b- relational operation a

== b - logical operation

func (a,b) - function call

4+21

a*(b + c/d)/20

q = 5*2 x =

++q % 3

q > 3

The operands can be constants, variables, or mixtures of the two, as you can see. Subexpressions are larger expressions that are combined to form some expressions. For instance, the sixth example's subexpression is c/d.

Every C expression has a value, which is a crucial characteristic of the language. You must carry out the operations in the sequence specified by operator precedence in order to determine the value.

Statements

A program's fundamental building components are statements. An application is made up of a number of sentences and any appropriate punctuation. An entire instruction to the computer is a statement. Statements in C are denoted by a semicolon at the conclusion. Therefore

legs = 4 is just an expression (which could be part of a larger expression), but legs = 4; is a statement.

What attributes do a complete instruction have? First, if you add a semicolon to any expression, C treats it as a statement. Those are what are known as expression statements. C won't object to lines like the following because of this:

8;

3 + 4;

These statements, however, serve no use for your programme and are not truly comprehensible. Statements often invoke functions and update values:

x = 25;

++x;

y = sqrt(x);

Not all full instructions are statements, even though a statement (or at least a logical statement) is a complete command. Think about the following assertion:

x = 6 + (y = 5);

Although it is simply a portion of the statement, the subexpression y = 5 in it is a complete command.

A semicolon is required to denote instructions that are in fact statements because a complete instruction is not always a statement.

Compound Statements (Blocks)

A compound statement, also known as a block, is made up of two or more statements that have been joined together and are enclosed in braces. An illustration of a while statement is provided below:

while (years < 100)

{

wisdom = wisdom * 1.05;

printf("%d %d\n", years, wisdom);

years = years + 1;

}

Any variable must be declared at the beginning of the block if it is to be used inside the block. Only within the block may variables that are declared inside be used.

CHAPTER 6 INPUT-OUTPUT IN C

When we say "input," we mean that we feed a programme with some data. This can be supplied either through the command line or as a file. The built-in functions of the C programming language allow you to read input and pass it along to the programme as needed.

The term "output" refers to the presentation of data on a screen, a printer, or in any other file. A collection of built-in functions in the C programming language are available to output the data on the computer screen.

The most popular functions for taking input and displaying output are printf() and scanf(), respectively. Let's look at an illustration:

```
#include <stdio.h>
int main()
{
//This is needed to run printf() function.
printf("C Programming");  //displays the content inside quotation
return 0;
}
```

Output:

C Programming

Explanation:

☐ Every program starts from main() function.

☐ A library function called printf() that displays output only functions if #includestdio.h> is included at the beginning.

☐ Standard input/output header file stdio.h is used in this case, and the #include command is used to paste the header file's code as needed. Compiler displays error when printf() function is encountered but stdio.h header file cannot be found.

☐ return 0; indicates the successful execution of the program.

Input- Output of integers in C

```
#include<stdio.h>
int main()
```

```c
{
int c=5;
printf("Number=%d",c);
return 0;
}
```
Output

Number=5

There is a conversion format string for integers called "%d" inside the quotation marks of the printf() function. If the conversion format string matches the last argument, which in this case is c, the value of c is shown.

```c
#include<stdio.h>
int main()
{
 int c;
printf("Enter a number\n");
scanf("%d",&c);
printf("Number=%d",c);
return 0;
}
```
Output

Enter a number

4

Number=4

To receive human input, use the scanf() function. The user is prompted for an input in this programme, and the value is then placed in variable c. Observe the '&' symbol before c. Value is kept at address c, which is indicated by the symbol &c.

Input- Output of floats in C

```c
#include <stdio.h>
int main()
{
```

```c
float a;
printf("Enter value: ");
scanf("%f",&a);
printf("Value=%f",a);
return 0;
//%f is used for floats instead of %d
}
```

Output

Enter value: 23.45

Value=23.450000

A variable's floating value is shown and inputted using the conversion format string "%f" for floats.

Input – Output of characters and ASCII code

```c
#include <stdio.h>
int main()
{
char var1;
printf("Enter character: ");
scanf("%c",&var1);
printf("You entered %c.",var1);
return 0;
}
```

Output

Enter character: g

You entered g.

Conversion format string "%c" is used in case of characters.

ASCII code:

In the programme mentioned above, when a character is entered, a numeric value (ASCII value) is instead stored. And that character is displayed when we use "%c" to display that value.

```c
#include <stdio.h>
int main()
```

```c
{
char var1;
printf("Enter character: ");
scanf("%c",&var1);
printf("You entered %c.\n",var1);
/* \n prints the next line(performs work of enter). */
printf("ASCII value of %d",var1);
return 0;
}
```

Output

Enter character:

g

103

When, 'g' is entered, ASCII value 103 is stored instead of g.

You can display character if you know ASCII code only. This is shown by following example.

```c
#include <stdio.h>
int main()
{
int var1=69;
printf("Character of ASCII value 69: %c",var1);
return 0;
}
```

Output

Character of ASCII value 69: E

The ASCII value of 'A' is 65, 'B' is 66 and so on to 'Z' is 90. Similarly ASCII value of 'a' is 97, 'b' is 98 and so on to 'z' is 122.

CHAPTER 7 FORMATTED INPUT-OUTPUT

A specific format for entering and displaying data is available. Improved results display can be achieved by format specifications.

Variations in Output for integer & floats:

```c
#include<stdio.h>
int main()
{
printf("Case 1:%6d\n",9876);
/*  Prints the number right justified within 6 columns  */
printf("Case 2:%3d\n",9876);
/* Prints the number to be right justified to 3 columns but, there are 4 digits so number is not right justified  */
printf("Case 3:%.2f\n",987.6543);
/* Prints the number rounded to two decimal places */
printf("Case 4:%.f\n",987.6543);
/* Prints the number rounded to 0 decimal place, i.e, rounded to integer */
printf("Case 5:%e\n",987.6543);
/* Prints the number in exponential notation (scientific notation) */
return 0;
}
```

Output

Case 1: 9876

Case 2:9876

Case 3:987.65

Case 4:988

Case 5:9.876543e+002

Variations in Input for integer and floats:

```c
#include <stdio.h>
int main()
{
```

```c
int a,b;
float c,d;
printf("Enter two intgers: ");
/*Two integers can be taken from user at once as below*/
scanf("%d%d",&a,&b);
printf("Enter intger and floating point numbers: ");
/*Integer and floating point number can be taken at once from user as below*/
scanf("%d%f",&a,&c);
return 0;
}
```
Similarly, any number of inputs can be taken at once from user.

EXERCISE:

1. To print out a and b given below, which of the following printf() statement will you use?

```c
#include<stdio.h>
float a=3.14;
double b=3.14;
```

A. printf("%f %lf", a, b);

B. printf("%Lf %f", a, b);

C. printf("%Lf %Lf", a, b);

D. printf("%f %Lf", a, b);

2. To scan a and b given below, which of the following scanf() statement will you use?

```c
#include<stdio.h>
float a;
double b;
```

A. scanf("%f %f", &a, &b);

B. scanf("%Lf %Lf", &a, &b);

C. scanf("%f %Lf", &a, &b);

D. scanf("%f %lf", &a, &b);

3. For a typical program, the input is taken using.

A. scanf

B. Files

C. Command-line

D. None of the mentioned

4. What is the output of this C code?

```c
#include <stdio.h>
int main()
{   int i = 10, j = 2;
printf("%d\n", printf("%d %d ", i, j));
}
```

A. Compile time error

B. 10 2 4

C. 10 2 2

D. 10 2 5

5. What is the output of this C code?

```c
#include <stdio.h>
int main()
{
int i = 10, j = 3;
printf("%d %d %d", i, j);
}
```

A. Compile time error

B. 10 3

C. 10 3 some garbage value

D. Undefined behavior

6. What is the output of this C code?

```c
#include <stdio.h>
int main()
{
```

}

int i = 10, j = 3, k = 3;

printf("%d %d ", i, j, k);

A. Compile time error

B. 10 3 3

C. 10 3

D. 10 3 somegarbage value

7. The syntax to print a % using printf statement can be done by.

A. %

B. %

C. '%'

D. %%

8. What is the output of this C code?

```c
#include <stdio.h>
int main()
{  int n;
scanf("%d", n);
printf("%d\n", n);
return 0;
}
```

A. Compilation error

B. Undefined behavior

C. Whatever user types

D. Depends on the standard

9. What is the output of this C code?

```c
#include <stdio.h>
int main()
{
short int i;
```

```c
scanf("%hd", &i);
printf("%hd", i);
return 0;
}
```

A. Compilation error

B. Undefined behavior

C. Whatever user types

D. None of the mentioned

10. In a call to printf() function the format specifier %b can be used to print binary equivalent of an integer.

A. True

B. False

11. Point out the error in the program?

```c
#include<stdio.h>
int main()
{
char ch;
int i;
scanf("%c", &i);
scanf("%d", &ch);
printf("%c %d", ch, i);
return 0;
}
```

A. Error: suspicious char to in conversion in scanf()

B. Error: we may not get input for second scanf() statement

C. No error

D. None of above

12. Which of the following is NOT a delimiter for an input in scanf?

A. Enter

B. Space

C. Tab

D. None of the mentioned

CHAPTER 8 OPERATORS

An operator is a symbol that instructs the compiler to carry out particular logical or mathematical operations. The built-in operators in the C programming language include the following categories:

* Arithmetic Operators
* Relational Operators
* Logical Operators
* Bitwise Operators
* Assignment Operators
* Increment and decrement operators
* Conditional operators
* Misc Operators

Arithmetic operator:

These are employed in the addition, subtraction, multiplication, division, and modulus operations in mathematics.

All of the C language's supported arithmetic operators are included in the table below. Suppose that variable A contains 10 and variable B contains 20. Then:

Operator

+

-

*

/

Description

Adds two operands

Subtracts second operand from the first

Multiplies both operands

Divides numerator by de-numerator

Example

A + B will give 30

A - B will give -10

A * B will give 200

B / A will give 2

%

++

--

Modulus Operator and remainder of after an integer division

Increments operator increases integer value by one

Decrements operator decreases integer value by one

B % A will give 0

A++ will give 11

A-will give 9

Relational Operators:

To compare the value of two variables, use these operations.

The relational operations supported by the C language are listed in the table below. If variable A has a value of 10 and variable B has a value of 20, then:

Operator	Description	Example
==	Checks if the values of two operands are equal or not, if yes	(A == B) is not
!=	Checks if the values of two operands are equal or not, if values are not equal then condition becomes true.	(A != B) is true.
>	Checks if the value of left operand is greater than the value of right operand, if yes then condition becomes true.	(A > B) is not true.
<	Checks if the value of left operand is less than the value of right operand, if yes then condition becomes true.	A < B) is true.

>=	Checks if the value of left operand is greater than or equal to the value of right operand, if yes then condition becomes true.	(A >= B) is not true.
<=	Checks if the value of left operand is less than or equal to the value of right operand, if yes then condition becomes true.	(A <= B) is true.

Logical Operators:

On the two provided variables, these operators are used to carry out logical operations.

The C language supports the logical operators listed in the following table. Suppose that variable A is 1 and variable B is 0, then:

Operator	**Description**	**Example**
&&	Called Logical AND operator. If both the operands are nonzero, then condition becomes true.	(A && B) is
||	Called Logical OR Operator. If any of the two operands is non-zero, then condition becomes true.	(A || B) is true.
!	Called Logical NOT Operator. Use to reverses the logical state of its operand. If a condition is true then Logical NOT operator will make false.	!(A && B) is true

Bitwise Operators

Bitwise operators operate bit-by-bit and work with bits. Programming at the bit level makes use of bitwise operators. While float and double cannot be operated upon by these operators, int and char may.

Showbits( ) Any numeric or character value's binary representation can be seen by using the function.

Bit wise operators in C language are; & (bitwise AND), | (bitwise OR), ~ (bitwise OR), ^ (XOR), << (left shift) and >> (right shift).

The truth tables for &, |, and ^ are as follows:

p	q	p & q	p | q	p ^ q
0	0	0	0	0
0	1	0	1	1
1	1	1	1	0
1	0	0	1	1

In the table below, the Bitwise operators that the C language supports are discussed. If variable A has a value of 60 (00111100) and variable B has a value of 13 (00001101), then:

Operator	Description	Example
&	Binary AND Operator copies a bit to the result if it	(A & B) will give 12, which is 0000 1100
|	Binary OR Operator copies a bit if it exists in either operand.	(A | B) will give 61, which is 0011 1101
^	Binary XOR Operator copies the bit if it is set in one operand but not both.	(A ^ B) will give 49, which is 0011 0001

Operator	Description	Example
~	Binary Ones Complement Operator is unary and has (~A) will give -61, which the effect of 'flipping' bits.	(~A) will give -61, which is 1100 0011 in 2's complement form.
<<	Binary Left Shift Operator. The left operands value is moved left by the number of bits specified by the right operand.	A << 2 will give 240 which is 1111 0000
>>	Binary Right Shift Operator. The left operands value is moved right by the number of bits specified by the right operand.	A >> 2 will give 15 which is 0000 1111

Assignment Operators:

In C programmes, assignment operators are used to assign values to the variables.

The C language supports the following assignment operators:

Operator	Description	Example
=	Simple assignment operator, Assigns values from right side operands to left side operand	C = A + B will assign value of A + B into C
+=	Add AND assignment operator, It adds right operand to the left operand and assign the result to left operand	C += A is equivalent to C = C + A
-=	Subtract AND assignment operator, It subtracts right operand from the left operand and assign the result to left operand	C -= A is equivalent to C = C - A

*=	Multiply AND assignment operator, It multiplies right operand with the left operand and assign the result to left operand	C *= A is equivalent to C = C * A
/=	Divide AND assignment operator, It divides left operand with the right operand and assign the result to left operand	C /= A is equivalent to C = C / A
%=	Modulus AND assignment operator, It takes modulus using two operands and assign the result to left operand	C %= A is equivalent to C = C % A
<<=	Left shift AND assignment operator	C <<= 2 is same as C = C << 2
>>=	Right shift AND assignment operator	C >>= 2 is same as C = C >> 2
&=	Bitwise AND assignment operator	C &= 2 is same as C = C & 2
^=	bitwise exclusive OR and assignment operator	C ^= 2 is same as C = C ^ 2
|=	bitwise inclusive OR and assignment operator	C |= 2 is same as C = C | 2

CHAPTER 9 : INCREMENT AND DECREMENT OPERATOR

The terms "increment operator" and "decrement operator" are used in C, respectively. These two operators are both unary, meaning they only have one operand. ++ adds 1 to the operand, while - deducts 1 from the operand. For instance:

Let a=5 and b=10

a++;

a--;

//a becomes 6

//a becomes 5

++a;   //a becomes 6

--a;   //a becomes 5

If ++ is used as a postfix (like in the expression var++), the operator will first return the value of the operand and only then increase it. If i++ is used as a prefix (like in the expression ++var), ++var will increment the value of var and then return it. This can be shown by the following illustration:

```
#include <stdio.h>
int main()
{
int c=2,d=2;
printf("%d\n",c++); //this statement displays 2 then, only c incremented by 1 to 3.
Printf("%d",++c);   //this statement increments 1 to c then, only c is displayed.
Return 0;
}
```

Output

2

4

Conditional Operators (? :)

In C programming, conditional operators are used to make decisions, i.e., to execute various statements based on the test condition and whether it is true or not.

Syntax of conditional operators;

conditional_expression?expression1:expression2

Expression1 is returned if the test condition is true (i.e., if its value is non-zero), while expression2 is returned if it is false.

Let's use a few instances to assist us grasp this:

int x, y ;

scanf ("%d", &x) ;

y = (x> 5 ? 3 : 4) ;

This statement will store 3 in y if x is greater than 5, otherwise it will store 4 in y.

The equivalent if statement will be,

if (x > 5)

y = 3 ;

else

y = 4 ;

Misc Operators:

There are few other operators supported by c language.

Operator	Description	Example
sizeof()	It is a unary operator which is used in sizeof(a), where a is integer, will finding the size of data type, constant, return 4. arrays, structure etc.	sizeof(a), where a is integer, will return 4.
&	Returns the address of a variable.	&a; will give actual address of the variable.
*	Pointer to a variable.	*a; will pointer to a variable.

Operators Precedence in C

The arrangement of terms in an expression is determined by operator precedence. This has an impact on how an expression is assessed. The multiplication operator has higher precedence than the addition operator, for example, but certain operators have higher precedence than others.

For instance, x = 7 + 3 * 2; in this case, x is given the value 13, not 20, because operator * has higher precedence than operator +. As a result, x is multiplied by 3*2 first, and then added to 7, giving the result 7.

In this table, the operators with the highest precedence are displayed at the top and those with the lowest precedence are displayed at the bottom. Higher precedence operators will be evaluated first within an expression.

Category	Operator	Associativity
Postfix	() [] -> . ++ - -	Left to right
Unary	+ - ! ~ ++ - - (type)* &sizeof	Right to left
Multiplicative	* / %	Left to right
Additive	+ -	Left to right
Shift	<<>>	Left to right
Relational	<<= >>=	Left to right
Equality	== !=	Left to right
Bitwise AND	&	Left to right
Bitwise XOR	^	Left to right
Bitwise OR	|	Left to right
Logical AND	&&	Left to right
Logical OR	||	Left to right
Conditional	?:	Right to left
Assignment	= += -= *= /= %=>>= <<= &= ^= |=	Right to left
Comma	,	Left to right

CHAPTER 10 CONTROL STATEMENTS

In C, programmes run consecutively in the order that they are displayed. This condition is not always true. On occasion, we might need to run a certain section of the programme. Additionally, it is possible that we will want to repeat the same step. We can set the order in which the program's various instructions are to be performed using control statements. They specify how control is passed on to different programme components. The following categories are used to categorise control statements:

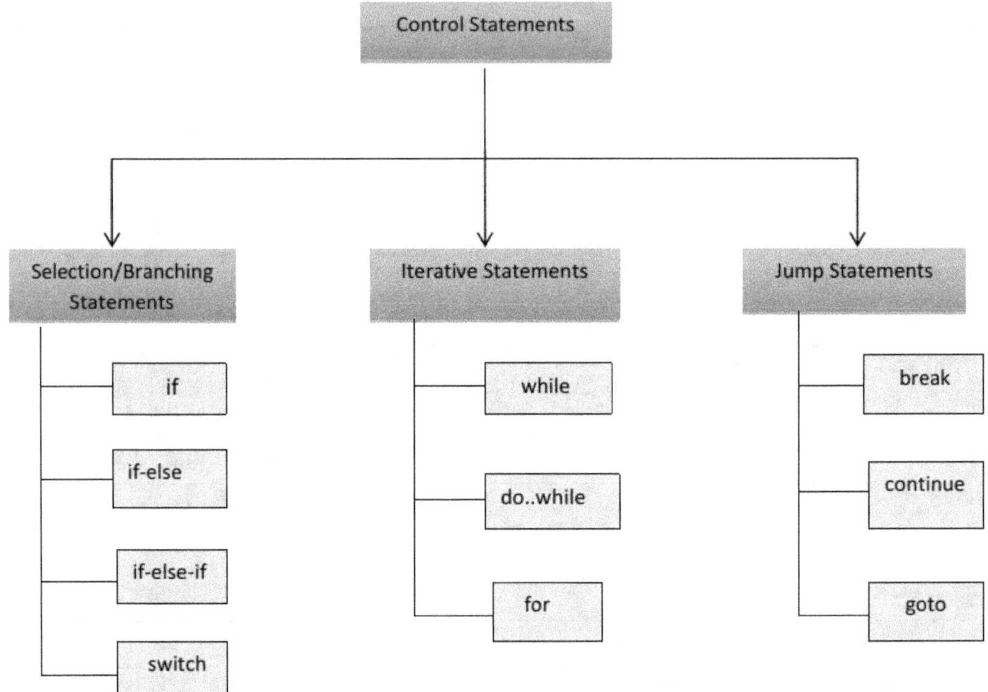

Fig: 1 Classification of control statements

SELECTION STATEMENTS

The branching or decision control statements are another name for the selection statements.

Introduction to Decision Control Statements

We occasionally run into situations where we must decide something. For instance, if it's sunny outside, I'll go outside and play; otherwise, I'll be at home. The type of weather in this situation determines my plan of action. I can go outside and play if it's sunny, but else I have to stay inside. Out of two alternatives, I select one. The same can be said for circumstances where we must choose from a variety of options. To put this theory into practise in computer programming, we have decision control statements.

Programmers must define one or more conditions that will be evaluated or tested by the programme, along with a statement or statements that will be executed if the condition is true, and optionally, additional statements that will be executed if the condition is false.

if Statement

The compiler is informed that a decision control instruction is about to follow by the keyword "if." We may incorporate decision-making into our programmes thanks to the if statement. Fig. 2 depicts the if statement's generic form.

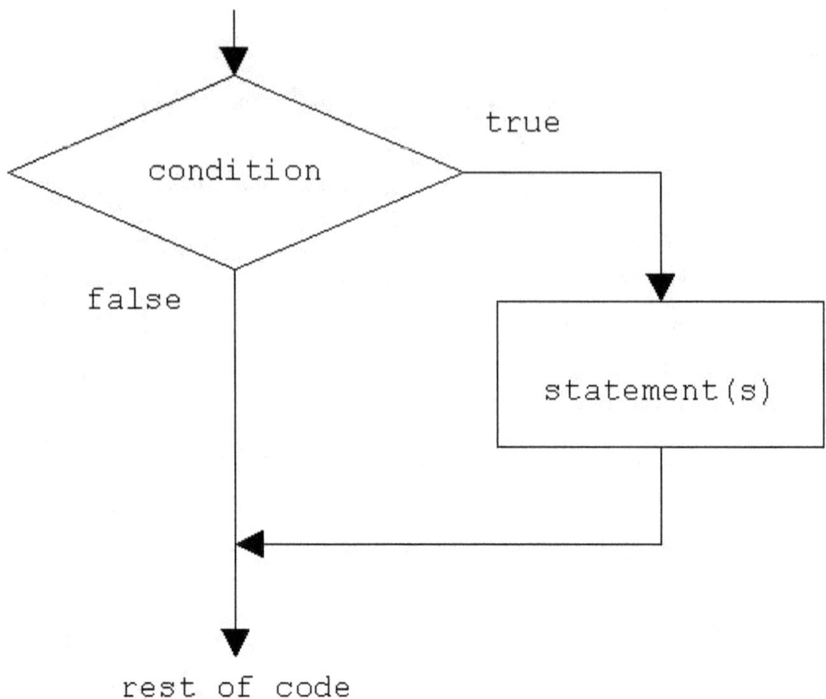

Fig 2: if statement construct

Syntax of if statement:

if (condition)

{

Statement 1;

…………..

Statement n;

}

//Rest of the code

The statement will be executed if the condition is true (nonzero). The statement won't be carried out if the condition is true(0). Consider the situation when we are creating a billing programme.

if (total_purchase >=1000)

printf("You are gifted a pen drive.\n");

Multiple statements may be grouped by putting them inside curly braces {}. For example:

```c
if (total_purchase>=1000)
{
gift_count++;
printf("You are gifted a pen drive.\n");
}
```

The statements enclosed in are typically indented for readability. The programmer can rapidly determine which statements need to be conditionally executed thanks to this. We'll see later how incorrect indentation can produce programmes that are confusing and challenging to interpret.

Programs:

1. Write a program to print a message if negative no is entered.

```c
#include<stdio.h>
int main()
{
int no;
printf("Enter a no : ");
scanf("%d", &no);
if(no<0)
{
printf("no entered is negative");
no = -no;
}
printf("value of no is %d \n",no);
return 0;
}
```

Output

Enter a no: 6

value of no is 6

Output

Enter a no: -2

value of no is 2

2. Write a program to perform division of 2 nos

```c
#include<stdio.h>
int main()
{
int a,b;
float c;
printf("Enter 2 nos : ");
scanf("%d %d", &a, &b);
if(b == 0)
{
printf("Division is not possible");
}
c = a/b;
printf("quotient is %f \n",c);
return 0;
}
```

Output:

Enter 2 nos: 6 2

quotient is 3

Output:

Enter 2 nos: 6 0

Division is not possible

if-else Statement

When the expression that comes after the if statement evaluates to true, the if statement alone will execute a single statement or a collection of statements. In the event that the expression evaluates to false, we use else to execute another set of statements.

```c
if (a > b)
{ z = a;
printf("value of z is :%d",z);
}
else
{ z = b;
```

printf("value of z is :%d",z);

}

'If block' refers to the collection of statements that follow the if. Similar to the else, the statements that follow it make up the "else block."

Programs:

3. Write a program to check whether the given no is even or odd

```c
#include<stdio.h>
int main()
{
int n;
printf("Enter an integer\n");
scanf("%d",&n);
if ( n%2 == 0 )
printf("Even\n");
else
printf("Odd\n");
return 0;
}
```

Output

Enter an integer 3

Odd

Output

Enter an integer 4

Even

4. Write a program to check whether a given year is leap year or not

```c
#include <stdio.h>
int main()
{
int year;
printf("Enter a year to check if it is a leap year\n");
```

```c
scanf("%d", &year);
if ( (year%4 == 0) && (( year%100 != 0) || ( year%400 == 0 ))
printf("%d is a leap year.\n", year);
else
printf("%d is not a leap year.\n", year);
return 0;
}
```

Output

Enter a year to check if it is a leap year 1996

1996 is a leap year

Output

Enter a year to check if it is a leap year 2015

2015 is not a leap year

Nested if-else

Either the body of the if statement or the body of an otherwise statement can include an entire if-else construct. 'Nesting' ifs is the term for doing this. The structure that follows demonstrates this.

```c
if (n > 0)
{
if (a > b)
z = a;
}
else
z = b;
```

The first if statement has the second if construct nested inside of it. The second if statement's condition is only checked if the first if statement's condition is satisfied. If it is untrue, the otherwise statement is carried out.

Program:

5. Write a program to check for the relation between 2 nos

```c
#include <stdio.h>
int main()
```

```c
{
int m=40,n=20;
if ((m >0 ) && (n>0))
{
printf("nos are positive");
if (m>n)
{
printf("m is greater than n");
}
else
{
printf("m is less than n");
}
}
else
{
printf("nos are negative");
}
return 0;
}
```

Output

40 is greater than 20

else-if Statement:

Writing a multi-way decision using this series of if statements is the most encompassing approach. The expressions are evaluated in order, and if any of them are true, the statement that goes along with them is performed, which ends the chain as a whole. Every statement's code is always either a single statement or a collection of them enclosed in braces.

If (expression)

statement

else if (expression)

statement

else if (expression)

statement

else if (expression)

statement

else

statement

When none of the other requirements are met, the last other element deals with the "none of the above" or default case. The trailing can be ignored or utilised for error checking to catch "impossible" conditions when there isn't an explicit action for the default in some cases.

Program:

6. The above program can be used as an eg here.

```c
#include <stdio.h>
int main()
{
int m=40,n=20;
if (m>n)
{
printf("m is greater than n");
}
else if(m<n)
{
printf("m is less than n");
}
else
{
printf("m is equal to n");
}
}
```

Output

m is greater than n

switch case:

This organisation makes it easier to choose from the many options. The switch statement is a multi-way decision that branches based on whether an expression matches one of several constant integer values [3].

```
switch(integer expression)
{
case constant 1 :
do this;
case constant 2 :
do this ;
case constant 3 :
do this ;
default :
do this ;
}
```

Any C expression that will produce an integer value is the integer expression that comes after the keyword switch. It could be an expression that evaluates to an integer or an integer constant like 1, 2, or 3. If an expression value meets a case, that case is where execution begins. Case expressions must all be unique. If none of the other conditions are satisfied, the default case is carried out. A default is optional; if neither it nor any of the circumstances match, nothing happens at all. Cases and the default provision may happen in any sequence.

Consider the following program:

```
main( )
{
int i = 2; switch
( i )
{
case 1:
```

```c
printf ( "I am in case 1 \n" ) ;
case 2:
printf ( "I am in case 2 \n" ) ;
case 3:
printf ( "I am in case 3 \n" ) ;
default :
printf ( "I am in default \n" ) ; }
}
```

Output

```
I am in case 2
I am in case 3
I am in default
```

The software prints case 2 and case 3 as well as the default case here. It is up to you to use a break statement to exit the switch immediately if you only want case 2 to be run.

```c
main( )
{
int i = 2 ;
switch ( i )
{
case 1:
printf ( "I am in case 1 \n" ) ;
break ;
case 2:
printf ( "I am in case 2 \n" ) ;
break ;
case 3:
printf ( "I am in case 3 \n" ) ;
break ;
default:
printf ( "I am in default \n" ) ;
}
```

}

The output of this program would be:

I am in case 2

Program

7. WAP to enter a grade & check its corresponding remarks.

```c
#include <stdio.h>
int main ()
{
char grade;
printf("Enter the grade");
scanf("%c", &grade);
switch(grade)
{
case 'A' :printf("Outstanding!\n" );
break;
case 'B' : printf("Excellent!\n" );
break;
case 'C' :printf("Well done\n" );
break;
case 'D' : printf("You passed\n" );
break;
case 'F' : printf("Better try again\n" );
break;
default :  printf("Invalid grade\n" );
}
printf("Your grade is  %c\n", grade );
return 0;
}
```

Output

Enter the grade

B

Excellent

Your grade is B

CHAPTER 11 ITERATIVE STATEMENTS

while statement

When the programme needs to carry out repeated actions, the while statement is employed. While statements generally take the following form:

while (condition) statement:

The statement inside the while loop will be continually executed by the programme until the condition is false(0). (The statement won't be carried out if the initial condition is false.)

Take into account the programme below:

```c
main( )
{
int p, n, count;
float r, si;
count = 1;
while ( count <= 3 )
{
printf ( "\nEnter values of p, n and r " ) ;
scanf("%d %d %f", &p, &n, &r ) ;
si=p * n * r / 100 ;
printf ( "Simple interest = Rs. %f", si ) ;
count = count+1;
}
}
```

Some outputs of this program:

Enter values of p, n and r 1000 5 13.5

Simple Interest = Rs. 675.000000

Enter values of p, n and r 2000 5 13.5

Simple Interest = Rs. 1350.000000

Enter values of p, n and r 3500 5 13.5

Simple Interest = Rs. 612.000000

All statements after the while are run three times by the programme. The 'body' of the while loop is made up of these sentences. A condition is contained in the brackets following the while. All statements contained in the while loop's body are repeatedly performed as long as this condition is true.

Consider the following program;

```c
/* This program checks whether a given number is a palindrome or not */
#include <stdio.h>
int main()
{
int n, reverse = 0, temp;
printf("Enter a number to check if it is a palindrome or not\n");
scanf("%d",&n);
temp = n;
while( temp != 0 )
{
reverse = reverse * 10;
reverse = reverse +temp%10;
temp = temp/10;
}
if ( n == reverse )
printf("%d is a palindrome number.\n", n);
else
printf("%d is not a palindrome number.\n", n);
return 0;
}
```

Output:

Enter a number to check if it is a palindrome or not

12321

12321 is a palindrome

Enter a number to check if it is a palindrome or not

12000

12000 is not a palindrome

do-while Loop

The do-while's body runs at least once. The relationship test happens at the bottom (as opposed to top) of the loop in the do-while structure, whereas it happens at the top of the while loop. This guarantees that the loop's body runs at least once. The body of the loop continues to run as long as the test is True since the do-while checks for a positive relationship test.

The format of the do-while is

do

{ block of one or more C statements; }

while (test expression)

The test expression needs to be enclosed in brackets, exactly like a while statement does.

Consider the following program

```c
// C program to add all the numbers entered by a user until user enters 0.
#include <stdio.h>
int main()
{   int sum=0,num;
do
{
/* Codes inside the body of do...while loops are at least executed once. */
printf("Enter a number\n");
scanf("%d",&num);
sum+=num;
}
while(num!=0);
printf("sum=%d",sum);
return 0;
}
```

Output:

Enter a number

3

Enter a number

-2

Enter a number

0

sum=1

Consider the following program:

```c
#include <stdio.h>
main()
{
int i = 10;
do
{
printf("Hello %d\n", i );
i = i -1;
}while ( i > 0 );
}
```

Output:

Hello 10

Hello 9

Hello 8

Hello 7

Hello 6

Hello 5

Hello 4

Hello 3

Hello 2

Hello 1

Program:

8. Program to count the no of digits in a number

```c
#include <stdio.h>
int main()
{
int n,count=0;
printf("Enter an integer: ");
scanf("%d", &n);
do
{
n/=10;
count++;
} while(n!=0);
/* n=n/10 */
printf("Number of digits: %d",count);
}
```

Output

Enter an integer: 34523

Number of digits: 5

for Loop

The most common looping instruction is for. The following is the general form of the for statement:

```c
for ( initialise counter ; test counter ; Updating counter )
{
do this;
and this;
and this;
}
```

Three details about a loop can be specified using the for in a single line:

(a) Setting a loop counter to zero (optional).

(b) Checking the loop counter to see if it has reached the necessary number of repetitions.

(c) Changing the loop counter's value by incrementing or decrementing.

Consider the following program

```c
int main(void)
{
int num;
printf("    n   n cubed\n");
for (num = 1; num <= 6; num++)
printf("%5d %5d\n", num, num*num*num);
return 0;
}
```

The program prints the integers 1 through 6 and their cubes.

```
n   n cubed
1
2
3
4
5
6
1
8
27
64
125
216
```

The first line of the for loop provides all the details about the loop parameters, including the initial value of num, the ultimate value of num, and the rate of increase of num [5].

The three parts of a for loop are expressions grammatically speaking. All three sections may be omitted, but the semicolons must always be present.

Consider the following program:

```c
main( )
{
int i ;
for ( i = 1 ; i <= 10 ; )
```

```c
{
printf ( "%d\n", i ) ;
i = i + 1 ;
}
}
```

In this case, the increment is carried out within the for loop's body rather than in the for statement. Note that despite this, the condition must be followed by a semicolon.

Programs:

st

9. Program to print the sum of 1   N natural numbers.

```c
#include <stdio.h>
int main()

{
int n,i,sum=0;
printf("Enter the limit: ");
scanf("%d", &n);
for(i=1;i<=n;i++)
{
sum = sum +i;
}
printf("Sum of N natural numbers is: %d",sum);
}
```

Output

Enter the limit: 5

Sum of N natural numbers is 15.

10. Program to find the reverse of a number

```c
#include<stdio.h>
int main()
{
```

```c
int num,r,reverse=0;
printf("Enter any number: ");
scanf("%d",&num);
for(;num!=0;num=num/10)
{
r=num%10;
reverse=reverse*10+r;
}
printf("Reversed of number: %d",reverse);
return 0;
}
```

Output:

Enter any number: 123

Reversed of number: 321

NESTING OF LOOPS

The C programming language permits the use of loops inside of loops. A few examples are provided in the section below to help demonstrate the idea.

Syntax:

The syntax for a nested for loop statement in C is as follows:

```c
for ( init; condition; increment )
{
for ( init; condition; increment)
{
statement(s);
}
statement(s);
}
```

The syntax for a nested while loop statement in C programming language is as follows:

```c
while(condition)
{
while(condition)
```

```c
{
statement(s);
}
statement(s);
}
```

The following is the syntax for a C programming language nested do...while loop statement:

```c
do
{
statement(s);
do
{
statement(s);
}
while(condition);
}
while(condition);
```

One last thing to keep in mind about loop nesting is that any form of loop can be placed inside of another type of loop.

A while loop or a for loop, for instance, might be placed inside the other.

Programs:

11. program using a nested for loop to find the prime numbers from 2 to 20:

```c
#include <stdio.h>
int main ()
{
/* local variable definition */
int i, j;
for(i=2; i<20; i++)
{
for(j=2; j <= (i/j); j++)
if(!(i%j))
break; // if factor found, not prime
}
```

```c
if(j > (i/j)) printf("%d is prime\n", i);
}
return 0;
}
```

Output:

2 is prime

3 is prime

5 is prime

7 is prime

11 is prime

13 is prime

17 is prime

19 is prime

12.
```
*
***
*****
*******
*********
```

```c
#include <stdio.h>
int main()
{
int row, c, n,I, temp;
printf("Enter the number of rows in pyramid of stars you wish to see ");
scanf("%d",&n);
temp = n;
for ( row = 1 ; row <= n ; row++ )
{
for ( i= 1 ; i < temp ; i++ )
{
printf(" ");
```

```c
temp--;
for ( c = 1 ; c <= 2*row - 1 ; c++ )
{
printf("*");
printf("\n");
}
}
}
return 0;
}
```

13. Program to print series from 10 to 1 using nested loops.

```c
#include<stdio.h>
void main ()
{
int a;
a=10;
for (k=1;k=10;k++)
{
while (a>=1)
{
}
a= 10;
}
}
```

Output:

10 9 8 7 5 4 3 2 1

10 9 8 7 5 4 3 2 1

10 9 8 7 5 4 3 2 1

10 9 8 7 5 4 3 2 1

10 9 8 7 5 4 3 2 1

10 9 8 7 5 4 3 2 1

```c
10 9 8 7 5 4 3 2 1
10 9 8 7 5 4 3 2 1
10 9 8 7 5 4 3 2 1
10 9 8 7 5 4 3 2 1
printf ("%d",a);
a--;
printf("\n");
```

CHAPTER 12 JUMP STATEMENTS

The break Statement

Just like from switch, the break statement allows an early exit from for, while, and do. The innermost enclosing loop or switch is instantly evacuated in response to a break. Any loop that encounters a break automatically moves control to the first statement after the break.

Consider the following example;

```
main( )
{
int i = 1 , j = 1 ;
while ( i++ <= 100 )
{
while ( j++ <= 200 )
{
if ( j == 150 )
break ;
else
printf ( "%d %d\n", i, j );
}
}
}
```

Because break is positioned inside the inner while in this programme, when j = 150, it only moves control outside the inner while.

The continue Statement

The next iteration of the enclosing for, while, or do loop begins when you use the continue statement, which is similar to the break statement but less frequently used. This indicates that the test portion is immediately executed in the while and do statements; in the for statement, control is transferred to the increment step. Switch does not use the continue statement; only loops do.

Consider the following program:

```
main( )
```

```c
{
int i, j ;
for ( i = 1 ; i <= 2 ; i++ )
{
for ( j = 1 ; j <= 2 ; j++ )
{
if ( i == j)
continue ;
printf ( "\n%d %d\n", i, j ) ;
}
}
}
```

The output of the above program would be...

1 2

2 1

Keep in mind that the continue statement transfers control to the for loop (inner) by sending the remaining statements that are waiting to be executed there when the value of I equals that of j.

The goto statement

The goto statement is described as "infinitely abusable" by Kernighan and Ritchie, who advise that it "be used rarely, if at all.

The goto statement instructs your programme to skip the subsequent statement in sequence and jump to a different place. The goto statement is formatted as follows:

goto statement label;

Consider the following program fragment

```c
if (size > 12)
goto a;
goto b;
a: cost = cost * 1.05;
flag = 2;
b: bill = cost * flag;
```

Here, the programme jumps to the block labelled as a: if the if conditions are satisfied; else, it moves to the block tagged as b:.

Exercise questions:

1. Use WAP to input a triangle's three sides and output the corresponding type.

2. Use WAP to enter the salesperson's name and the total amount of sales he generated. Determine the commission earned and print it.

TOTAL SALES

1-1000

1001-4000

6001-6000

6001 and above

3. WAP to calculate the wages of a labor.

TIME

First 10 hrs.

Next 6 hrs.

Next 4 hrs.

Above 10 hrs.

RATE OF COMMISSION

3 %

8 %

12 %

15 %

WAGE

Rs 60

Rs 15

Rs 18

Rs 25

4. Depending on the user's preference, WAP will compute the area of a triangle, circle, square, or rectangle.

5. WAP that will print various formulae & do calculations:

i. Vol of a cube

ii. Vol of a cuboid

iii. Vol of a cyclinder

iv. Vol of sphere

6. WAP to print the following series

i. $1 + 1/2 + 1/3 \ldots\ldots 1/10$

ii. $P = (1*2) + (2*3) + (3*4) + \ldots\ldots(8*9) + (9*10)$

iii. $Q = \frac{1}{2} + \frac{3}{4} + 5/6 + \ldots 13/14$

iv. $S = 2/5 + 5/9 + 8/13 \ldots n$

v. $S = x + x\ + x\ + x \ldots + x\ + x$

vi. $P = x + x\ /3 + x\ /5 + x\ /7 \ldots\ldots\ldots n$ terms

vii. $S = (13*1) + (12*2) \ldots(1*13)$

viii. $S = 1 + 1/(2\ ) + 1/(3\ ) + 1/(4\ ) + 1/(5\ )$

ix. $S = 1/1! + 1/2! + 1/3! \ldots\ldots + 1/n!$

x. $S = 1 + 1/3! + 1/5! + \ldots\ldots n$ terms

xi. $S = 1 + (1+2) + (1+2+3) + (1+2+3+4) \ldots\ldots\ldots + (1+2+3 \ldots\ldots 20)$

xii. $S = x + x\ /2! + x\ /3! + x\ /4! \ldots + x\ /10!$

xiii. $P = x/2! + x\ /3! + \ldots\ldots x\ /10!$

xiv. $S = 1 - 2 + 3 - 4 \ldots\ldots + 9 - 10$

xv. $S = 1 - 2\ + 3\ - 4 \ldots\ldots + 9\ - 10$

xvi. $S = 1/(1+2) + 3/(3+5) \ldots\ldots 15/(15+16)$

xvii. $S = 1 + x\ /2! - x\ /4! + x\ /6! \ldots n$

xviii. $S = 1 + (1+2) + (1+2+3) \ldots\ldots(1+2+3+4 \ldots\ldots 20)$

xix. $S = 1 + x + x\ /2 + x\ /3 \ldots\ldots + x\ /n$

xx. $S = 1*3/2*4*5\ + 2*4/3*5*6 + 3*5/4*6*7 \ldots\ldots n*(n+2)/(n+1)*(n+3)$
        $*(n+4)$

7. WAP to input a no & print its corresponding table.

8. WAP to print the table from 1 to 10 till 10 terms.

9. WAP to input a no & print its factorial.

10. WAP to input a no & check whether it is prime or not.

11. WAP to input a no & print all the prime nos upto it.

12. WAP to input a no & print if the no is perfect or not.

13. WAP to find the HCF of 2 nos.

14. Within 100, WAP should output the Pythagorean triplets. Three positive numbers a, b, and c make up a Pythagorean triplet if they can be combined to equal c.

15. WAP to enter a no and determine whether it is automorphic. A number is considered automorphic if its square "ends" in the same digits as the number itself. As an illustration, 5, 6, 76, and 890625 are all automorphic integers (5 = 25, 6 = 3, 76 = 5776, and 890625 = 793212890625).

16. WAP to convert a given no of days into years, weeks & days.

17. Use WAP to submit a no and determine whether it is an Armstrong no. An integer is considered an Armstrong number if the cubes of all of its digits added together equal the number itself. For instance, the number 371 (because 3 + 7 + 1 = 371) is an Armstrong number.

18. In Jalandhar, bats, wickets, and balls are sold by a provider of cricket equipment. WAP to produce a sales invoice. Enter the date of purchase, the buyer's name, the price per item, and the quantity of each item into the console. Calculate the total selling value and add 17.5% sales tax if it exceeds $300,000, 12.5 % if it exceeds $150,000, and 7 % in all other cases. Show the whole sales total, the sales tax, and the total.

19. WAP to check whether a given number is magic number or not.

(What is a magic number? Example: 1729

- Find the sum of digits of the given number.(1 + 7 + 2 + 9 => 19)
- Reverse of digit sum output. Reverse of 19 is 91

2   2   2

2

2

2

3   3   3

20. Find the product of digit sum and the reverse of digit sum.(19 X 91 = 1729)

• If the value of the final product and the input are the same, the input is a magic number.(19 X 91 <=> 1729)

To find the general root of the given number, write a C programme. (In order to get the generic root of a number, we must first calculate the number's digit sum up to a single digit output. The generic no is the name given to the resulting no. Eg: 456791: 4+5+6+7+9+1=32. 3 +2 =5. 5 now serves as the general root of the specified no.

MODULE 2
CHAPTER 13 FUNCTION

MONOLITHIC VS MODULAR PROGRAMMING:

1. Monolithic programming refers to a huge programme that only has a single function.

2. Programmers can break up a large programme into smaller, independently produced, and tested modules with the use of modular programming. The linker will then connect each of these modules to create the full programme.

3. On the other hand, monolithic programming just has one thread of execution and does not partition the programme. When a programme grows in size, it becomes annoying and challenging to manage.

Disadvantages of monolithic programming:

1. Difficult to check error on large programs.

2. Difficult to maintain.

3. Code can be specific to a particular problem. i.e it cannot be reused.

Advantage of modular programming:

1. Modular program are easier to code and debug.

2. Reduces the programming size.

3. Code can be reused in other programs.

4. It is possible to isolate the issue to a single module, making it simpler to identify and fix the fault.

FUNCTION:

A function is a collection of sentences that work together to complete a goal. The default function in every C programme is main(), and even the simplest programmes can create additional functions.

Function Declaration OR Function Prototype:

1. It is also known as function prototype.

2. It inform the computer about the three things

a)   Name of the function

b)   Number and type of arguments received by the function.

c)   Type of value return by the function

Syntax:

return_type function_name (type1 arg1 , type2 arg2);

OR

return_type function_name (type1 type2);

3. Information about the called function is required when calling a function. The declaration is not required if the called function comes before the calling function.

Function Definition:

1. It consists of code description and code of a function.

It consists of two parts

a) Function header

b) Function coding

The I/O function definition explains what it does and how it works.

Syntax:

return_type function_name (type1 arg1 , type2 arg2)

```
{
local variable;
statements;
return (expression);
}
```

2. Function definition can be positioned wherever you choose in the programme, however it is typically put after the main function.

3. Declared inside a function, a local variable is exclusive to that function. It only exists within the function and cannot be utilised anywhere else in the programme.

4. Function definition cannot be nested.

5. When the return type is missing, it is automatically presumed to be an integer. Return type indicates the kind of value that function will return.

USER DEFINE FUNCTIONS VS STANDARD FUNCTION:

User Define Function:

If user-defined functions are those that the user declares, calls, and defines. Each user-defined function consists of three components:

1. Prototype or Declaration

2. Calling

3. Definition

Standard Function:

For typical activities like input/output and processing character strings, the C standard library is a standardised collection of header files and library routines. Since C lacks built-in keywords for these activities, unlike other languages (such COBOL, FORTRAN, and PL/I), practically all C programmes rely on the standard library to run.

CHAPTER 14 FUNCTION CATAGORIES

There are four main categories of the functions these are as follows:

1. Function with no arguments and no return values.

2. Function with no arguments and a return value.

3. Function with arguments and no return values.

4. Function with arguments and return values.

Function with no arguments and no return values:

syntax:

void funct (void);

main ( )

{

funct ( );

}

void funct (void);

{

}

NOTE: Between calling and called functions, there is no communication. Functions run separately, reading data and printing results in the same block.

Example:

void link (void) ;

int main ()

{

link ();

}

void link (void);

{

printf (" link the file ")

}

Function with no arguments and a return value: These functions only have a return value instead of any arguments.

example:

```
int msg (void) ;
int main ( )
{
int s = msg ( );
printf( "summation = %d" , s);
}
int msg ( void )
{
int a, b, sum ;
sum = a+b ;
return (sum) ;
}
```

NOTE: This independently run function reads the value from the keyboard, initialises, and returns a value. There is some communication between calling and called functions.

Function with arguments and no return values:

Since there are arguments in these functions, the calling function sends data to the called function, but the called function does not return anything. Such functions partially rely on the function they are called from, and the result is used by the called function.

Example:

```
void  msg ( int , int );
int main ( )
{
int a,b;
a= 2; b=3;
msg( a, b);
}
void msg ( int a , int b)
{
```

int s ;

sum = a+b;

printf ("sum = %d" , s) ;

}

Function with arguments and return value:

Here, the called function receives arguments that were supplied to it and returns a value to the calling function.

example:

```c
int  msg ( int , int ) ;
int main ( )
{
int a, b;
a= 2; b=3;
int s = msg (a, b);
printf ("sum = %d" , s ) ;
}
int msg( int a , int b)
{
int sum ;
sum =a+b ;
return (sum);
}
```

CHAPTER 15 ACTUAL ARGUMENTS AND FORMAL ARGUMENTS

Actual Arguments:

1. The calling function refers to the arguments that are mentioned in the function when it is called.

2. These values make up the function's real arguments when it is invoked.

It can be expressed as a function expression on any function call that returns a value using the syntax constant.

ex: funct (6,9) , funct (a,b)

Formal Arguments:

1. Dummy or formal arguments are those that are mentioned in the definition of the function.

2. Simply holding the value that the calling function sends is all that these parameters are utilised for.

3. Formal arguments are produced when a function call begins and discarded when the function is finished, just like other local variables of the function.

Basic difference between formal and local argument are:

a) Local variables are stated at the beginning, while formal arguments are declared within the ( ).

b) When a value of the actual argument is supplied, formal arguments are immediately initialised.

c) Whereas other local variables are assigned by using a statement inside the body of the function.

Note: It is important to match the order, number, and type of formal arguments in the function definition with the order, number, and type of actual parameters in the function call.

PARAMETER PASSING TECHNIQUES:

1. call by value
2. call by reference

Call by value:

Here, the formal arguments get the value of the actual arguments and perform the operation.

Any changes to the formal arguments have no impact on the actual arguments because they are a photocopy of the actual arguments.

When control returns to the calling function, changes made to the formal parameter t are lost since they are local to the block of the called function.

Example:

```
void swap (int a , int b)
{
int t;
t = a;
a=b;
b = t;
}
main( )
{
int k = 50,m= 25;
swap( k, m) ;
(k, m);
}
```

Output:

```
/* called function */
/ * calling function */ print
/ * calling function */
50, 25
```

Explanation:

int k= 50, m=25 ;

The first two memory spaces, designated as k and m, respectively store the numbers 50 and 25.

swap (k,m);

Control is transferred to the called function when this function is invoked.

Values are assigned to the 'a' and 'b' in the form of void swap (int a, int b), k, and m.

so if a=50 and b=25,

Following that, control enters the function, and when int t is performed, a temporary memory area, 't,' is generated.

t=a; Means the value of a is assigned to the t , then t= 50.

a=b; Here value of b is assigned to the a , then a= 25;

b=t; Again t value is assigned to the b , then b= 50;

Following this, the control returns to the main function and runs the print (k,m) function. It gives back a value of 50, 25.

NOTE:

The values in the calling function are unaffected by any changes made to the called function.

Call by reference:

Here, addresses or references are passed in place of values. Instead of values, use function operators or addresses.In this case, formal arguments serve as a guide to more substantive ones.

Example:

```c
#include<stdio.h>
void add(int *n);
int main()
{
int num=2;
printf("\n The value of num before calling the function=%d", num);
add(&num);
printf("\n The value of num after calling the function = %d", num);
return 0;
}
void add(int *n)
{
*n=*n+10;
printf("\n The value of num in the called function = %d", n);
}
```

Output:

Before calling the function, num was set to 2

The calling function's num parameter is set to 20. After running the function, the value of num is 20.

NOTE:

Any changes made to the called function have an impact on the values of the calling function when using the call by address approach.

EXAMPLES:

1: Write a function to return larger number between two numbers:

```
int fun(int p, int q)
{
int large;
if(p>q)
{
large = p;
}
else
{
large = q;
}
return large;
}
```

2: Write a program using function to find factorial of a number.

```
#include <stdio.h> int
factorial (int n)
{
int i, p;
p = 1;
for (i=n; i>1; i=i-1)
{
p = p * i;
}
return (p);
}
```

```c
void main()
{
int a, result;
printf ("Enter an integer number: ");
scanf ("%d", &a);
result = factorial (a);
printf ("The factorial of %d is %d.\n", a, result);
}
```

EXERCISE:

1. How would you define function?

2. Why do programmes utilise functions?

3. What do "call by value" and "call by address" mean?

4. What distinguishes persuasive arguments from formal arguments?

5. How many different kinds of functions are there in C?

6. How many arguments may a function take in?

7. Use one of the following to add two numbers:

a) with argument with return type;

b) with argument without return type;

c) without argument with return type.

8. To determine the factorial of a keyed-in number, create a programme using functions.

9. To determine the value of n raised to m, write the function power(n,m).

10. The user enters a year using the keyboard. To determine whether the year is a leap year or not, create a function.

11. Create a function that takes a number as an argument and outputs the number's multiplication table.

12. Create a programme to find a number's prime factors. Prime factors of 24, for instance, are 2, 2, 2, and 3, whereas those of 35 are 5 and 7.

13. Create a method that takes two arguments—a float and an int—from main(), calculates their product, and returns the result, which is reported by main().

14. Create a function that takes a list of percentage-based integers and outputs their sum, average, and standard deviation. Print the outcome in main() after calling this function.

15. Create a function that takes a student's scores from three topics and returns the average and percentage of those scores. Print the outcome in main() after calling this function.

16. Create a function to determine the digit sum of a user-inputted number.

17. Create a programme that uses a function to determine a number's binary equivalent.

18. Write a C function to evaluate the series

$\sin(x) = x - (x/3!) + (x/5!) - (x/7!) + \ldots$ to five significant digit.

19. If a triangle has p, q, and r as its three sides, then its area is given by 1/2 area = (S(S-p)(S-q)(S-r)) where S = (p+q+r)/2.

Using the formula above, create a computer programme that uses functions to determine the area of a triangle.

20. Write a function to calculate the GCD and LCM of two numbers.

21. Write a function that accepts a number as an input and outputs the number's product of digits.

22. Create a single function that can be used to output both friendly pairs and perfect numbers.(Two distinct numbers are said to be amicable if the product of their respective appropriate divisors equals the other.

The numbers 284 and 220 get along well.)

23. Write a function to find whether a character is alphanumeric.

CHAPTER 16: RECURSION

A method called recursion involves defining a problem in terms of itself. A function can be called from another function in the language "C." Recursive functions, in which the same function is called from within the body of another statement, are those that call themselves. 'Circular Definition' is a word that is frequently used to describe recursion. So, defining anything in terms of itself is the process of recursion. A function must be able to call itself in order to use the recursion approach in programming.

Example:

```
void main()
{

.........................
fun1();

.........................
} void
fun1()
{

.........................
/*RECURSIVE CALL*/

.........................
}
/* Some statements*/
/* Some statements */
/* Some statements */ fun1();
/* Some statements */
```

Fun1() is a recursive function in this case because it calls itself within the body of another function. The code of fun1() will be run when main() calls it, and since fun1() is called inside of another function, fun1() will also be executed. Although it appears that the aforementioned programme will run indefinitely, most recursive functions have a terminating condition that prevents further recursion. This is demonstrated by the following programme, which prints all numbers beginning with the provided number and decreasing by 1 each time:

```c
void main()
{
int a;
printf("Enter a number");
scanf("%d",&a);
fun2(a);
}
int fun2(int b)
{
printf("%d",b);
b--;
if(b>=1)   /* Termination condition i.e. b is less than 1*/
{
fun2(b);
}
}
```

How to write a Recursive Function?

It is required to define the solution of the problem in terms of a smaller problem of a similar type before constructing a recursive function for the larger problem.

The following are the two primary steps in writing a recursive function:

(i) Determine the non-recursive (base case) portion of the issue and how it can be resolved (the portion of the issue that can be resolved without recursion).

(ii). Determine the problem's recursive section (generic case), or the area where a recursive call will be made.

It is essential to identify the non-recursive component of the issue because without it, the function will keep calling itself, leading to infinite recursion.

How control flows in successive recursive calls?

The following example shows the control flow through a series of recursive calls:

Take a look at the following programme, which computes a number's factorial using recursive function.

```c
void main()
{
int n,f;
printf("Enter a number");
scanf("%d",&n);
f=fact(a);
printf("Factorial of %d is %d",n,f);
}
int fact(int m)
{
int a;
if (m==1)
return (1);
else
a=m*fact(m-1);
return (a);
}
```

The value of n is copied into m in the programme above if the user enters a value of 1, or n=1. The factorial of 1 is 1 because the condition 'if(m==1)' is satisfied and the value of m is 1. As a result, 1 is returned using the return statement.

The value of n is copied into m when the entered number is 2, or when n=2. Then, when the 'if(m==1)' condition in the function fact() fails, we come across the phrase a=m*fact(m-1), where recursion is introduced. The expression (m*fact(m-1)) is evaluated to (2*fact(1)) since m has a value of 2, and the result is stored in a(factorial of a). Since fact(1) returns a value of 1, the above statement becomes (2*1) or just 2. The result of the expression m*fact(m-1) is 2; it is then placed in the variable a and returned to main(). 'Factorial of 2 is 2' will be printed there.

If n=4 in the aforementioned programme, main() will call fact(4) and fact(4) will return the computed value, f, to main(). However, fact(4) will call fact(4-1) or fact(3) and wait for a value to be returned before sending back to main(). In a similar fashion, fact(3) will call fact(2), and so forth. Until m equals 1 and fact(1) is called, which yields a result known as the "termination condition," this series of calls continues. Therefore, we may state that what occurred for n=4 is as follows.

fact(4) returns (4*fact(3))

fact(3) returns (3*fact(2))

fact(2) returns (2*fact(1))

fact(1) returns (1)

So for **n**=4, the factorial of 4 is evaluated to 4*3*2*1=24.

For **n**=3, the control flow of the program is as follows:

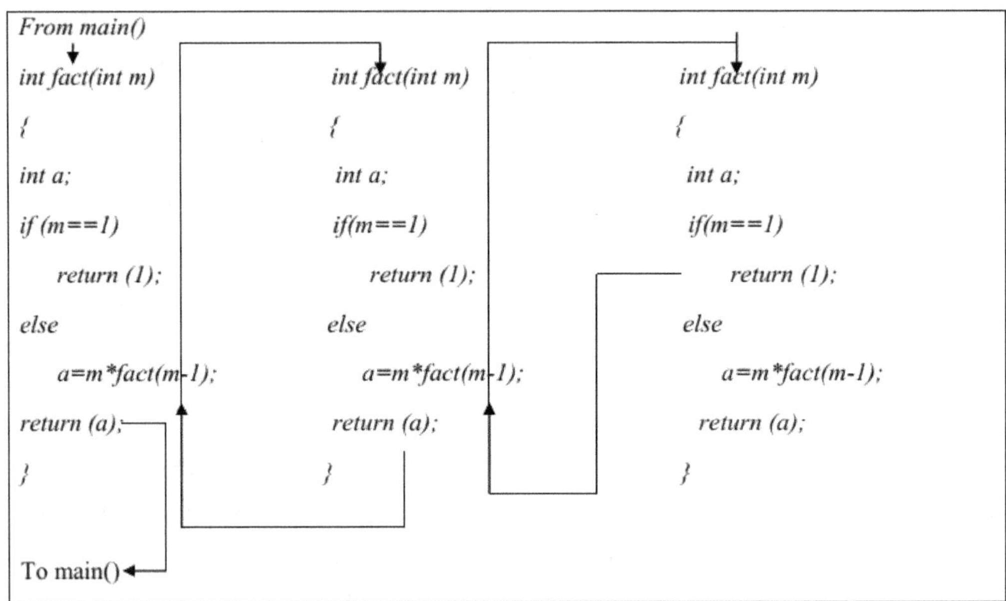

Winding and Unwinding phase

Every recursive function has two stages of operation: the winding phase and the unwinding phase. When the termination condition in a call becomes true, the winding phase comes to a close and no further calls to the recursive function are necessary. A function calls itself during this phase, and no return statements are executed.

Following the winding phase, the unwinding phase begins, and all calls to recursive functions begin returning in reverse order until the first instance of the function returns. During this stage, control loops back via each function instance.

Implementation of Recursion

We discovered that recursive calls operate just like regular function calls, negating the need for an additional mechanism to implement recursion. All function calls, whether they are recursive or not, are implemented using the run-time stack. A Last In First Out (LIFO) data structure is the stack. This indicates that the first item to be removed from the stack (POP Operation) will be the last item to be deposited there (PUSH Operation). Stack keeps track of a function's activation record (AR) as it runs. Here, we will use the factorial of a number function fact() from the previous recursive programme as an example.

Suppose fact() is called from main() with argument 3 i.e.

fact(3);   /*From main()*/

We'll now observe the run-time stack's changes while the factorial of 3 is evaluated.

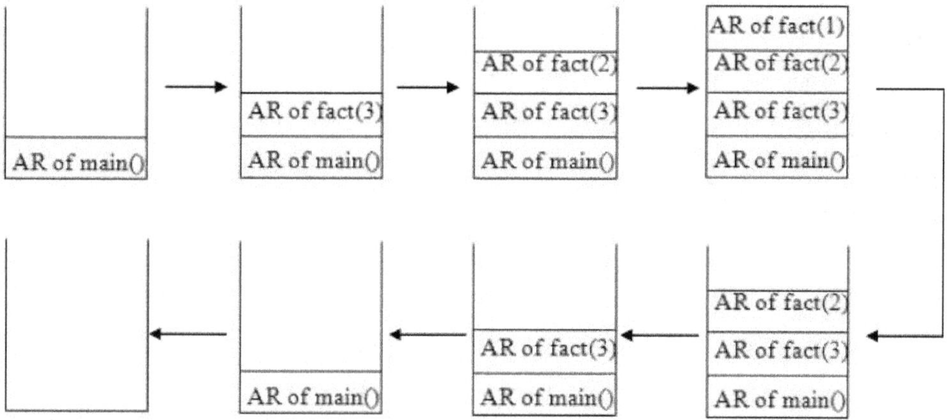

The actions that follow will show how the contents of the aforementioned stack were expressed: When main() is first called, the stack is pushed with the main() AR. Then fact(3) is called by main(), pushing fact(3)'s AR. Fact(2) is now being called by fact(3), therefore PUSH fact(2)'s AR into the stack. The same applies to PUSH AR of fact(1). After the aforementioned, POP fact(1)'s corresponding AR when fact(1) is finished. Likewise, POP a specific function's corresponding AR when a function is finished. So POP AR of main() when it has finished running. Stack is now empty.

As fresh Activation Records(AR) are generated and placed into the stack with each call to the function, the stack content rises during the winding phase. The Activation Records are popped from the stack in LIFO order during the unwinding phase until the originating call returns.

Examples of Recursion

Q1. Write a program using recursion to find the summation of numbers from 1 to n.

Ans: The statement "sum of numbers from 1 to n can be represented as sum of numbers from 1 to n- 1 plus n" can be used to express this.

Sum of numbers from 1 to n = n + Sum of numbers from 1 to n-1

= n + n-1 + Sum of numbers from 1 to n-2

= n+ n-1 + n-2 + ... +1

The program which implements the above logic is as follows:

```c
#include<stdio.h>
void main()
{
int n,s;
printf("Enter a number");
scanf("%d",&n);
s=sum(n);
printf("Sum of numbers from 1 to %d is %d",n,s);
}
int sum(int m) int r;
if(m==1)
return (1);
else
r=m+sum(m-1);/*Recursive Call*/
return r;
}
```

Output:

Enter a number 5

15

Q2. Write a program using recursion to find power of a number i.e. n.

Ans: We can write,

m

n_m

$= n*n_{m-1}$

$m-2$

$=n*n*n$

$=n*n*n*\ldots\ldots\ldots\ldots m \text{ times} *n$

$m-m$

The program which implements the above logic is as follows:

```c
#include<stdio.h>
int power(int,int);
void main()
{
int n,m,k;
printf("Enter the value of n and m");
scanf("%d%d",&n,&m);
k=power(n,m);
printf("The value of n   for n=%d and m=%d is %d",n,m,k);
}
int power(int x, int y)
{
if(y==0)
{
return 1;
}
else
{
return(x*power(x,y-1));
}
}
```

Output:

Enter the value of n and m

3

5

m

The value of n   for n=3 and m=5 is 243

m

Q3.Write a program to find GCD (Greatest Common Divisor) of two numbers.

Ans: The largest integer that divides both integers with a remainder of zero is known as the GCD or HCF (Highest Common Factor) of two integers. The Euclid's Remainder Algorithm, which claims that the GCD of two numbers, let's say x and y, is.

GCD(x, y) = **x**

if y is 0

= **GCD(y, x%y)** otherwise

The program which implements the previous logic is as follows:

```c
#include<stdio.h>
int GCD(int,int);
void main()
{
int a,b,gcd;
printf("Enter two numbers");
scanf("%d%d",&a,&b);
gcd=GCD(a,b);
printf("GCD of %d and %d is %d",a,b,gcd);
}
int GCD(int x, int y)
{
if(y==0)
return x;
else
return GCD(y,x%y);
}
```

Output:

Enter two numbers   21

35

GCD of 21 and 35 is 7

Q4: Write a program to print Fibonacci Series upto a given number of terms.

Ans: The Fibonacci series is a sequence of integers where the first two integers are 1 and each integer after the third is the sum of the two preceding integers, i.e.

1, 1, 2, 3, 5, 8, 13, 21, 34, 55, 89, ……........................

The program which implements the above logic is as follows:

```c
#include<stdio.h>
int Fibonacci(int);
void main()
```

```c
{
int term,i;
printf("Enter the number of terms of Fibonacci Series which is going to be printed");
scanf("%d",&term);
for(i=0;i<term;i++)
{
printf("%d",Fibonacci(i));
}
}
int Fibonacci(int x)
{
if(x==0 || x==1)
return 1;
else
return (Fibonacci(x-1) + Fibonacci(x-2));
}
```

Output:

Enter the number of terms of Fibonacci Series which is going to be printed 6

1 1 2 3 5 8 13

CHAPTER 17 RECURSION VERSES ITERATION

Every recurrent issue can be solved iteratively or recursively.

In cases where the issue is recursive, recursion should be used. If the issue isn't already recursive, iteration should be utilised.

Although recursive solutions have a higher execution cost than their iterative equivalents, they have the advantage of having very straightforward code.

Since PUSH and POP operations are needed, recursive versions of problems take longer to solve than iterative versions.

The same block of code is run repeatedly in both iteration and recursion, but repetition in iteration happens when the block of code is finished or a continue statement is encountered whereas repetition in recursion happens when a function calls itself.

Recursive problem solving is simpler to implement for complex issues than iterative approaches. Utilising an iterative version will eliminate recursion.

Tail Recursion

If the matching recursive call is the final statement to be executed inside the function, the recursive call is said to be tail recursive.

Example: Look at the following recursive function

```
void show(int a)
{
if(a==1)
return;
printf("%d",a);
show(a-1);
}
```

Since the recursive call in the aforementioned example occurs as the final statement of the function, it is referred to as a tail recursive call.

If the recursive call appears in the return statement and is not a component of an expression, it is said to be tail recursive in non-void functions (functions with return types other than void). Otherwise, it is said to be non-tail recursive. Take a look at the example int hcf(int p, int q) below.

```
{
if(q==0)
return p;
else
return(hcf(q,p%q));
}
int factorial(int a)
{
if(a==0)
return 1;
else
/*Tail recursive call*/
return(a*factorial(a-1));
}
/*Not a Tail recursive call*/
```

In the aforementioned example, the recursive call in hcf() is Tail recursive since it is not a component of the expression (i.e., the call is the expression in the return statement). However, the recursive call in factorial() is not a Tail excursive call because it is a component of the expression in the return statement (a*recursive call).

If all of a function's recursive calls are tail recursive, the function is said to be tail recursive.

Using loops, it is simple to build tail recursive functions, No action is left pending after the recursive call returns because with tail recursive functions, the final task a function does is a recursive call. Since there is nothing to be done in the unwinding phase of tail recursive functions, we can jump immediately from the last recursive call to the location where the recursive function was first called. Compilers are able to implement tail recursion effectively, thus we will always strive to make our recursive functions tail recursive whenever possible.

These types of functions must complete the outstanding work after the recursive call completes and are referred to as augmentive recursive functions if they are not tail recursive.

Indirect and Direct Recursion

This type of recursion is known as indirect recursion since the function fun1() is indirectly calling itself if a function fun1() calls another function fun2(), which in turn calls function fun1().

```
fun1( )
{
......................    /* Some statements*/
fun2();
......................    /* Some statements*/
}
fun2( )
{
......................    /* Some statements*/
fun1();
...................... /* Some statements*/
}
```

In indirect recursion, the function chain can contain any number of functions. As an illustration, let's say there are n functions, ranging from f1() to fn(), and they play the following roles: With fn() calling f1(), f1() calls f2(), f2() calls f3, f3() calls f4, and so on.

Direct recursion is referred to as when a function calls itself directly, for example, when fun1() is called inside the body of another function. Take a look at this as an illustration.

```
fun1()
{
...     /* Some statements*/
fun2();
...     /* Some statements*/
```

}

Indirect recursion is complex, so it is rarely used.

Exercise:

Find the output of programs from 1 to 5.

1. void main()

```
{
printf("%d\n",count(17243));
}
int count(int x)
{
if(x==0)
return 0;
else
return 1+count(x/10)
}
```

2. void main()

```
{
printf("%d\n",fun(4,8));
printf("%d\n",fun(3,8));
}
int fun(int x. int y)
{
if(x==y)
return x;
else
return (x+y+fun(x+1,y-1));
}
```

3. void main()

```
{
```

```c
printf("%d\n",fun(4,9));
printf("%d\n",fun(4,0));
printf("%d\n",fun(0,4));
}
int fun(int x, int y)
{
if(y==0)
return 0;
if(y==1)
return x;
return x+fun(x,y-1);
}


4. void main()
{
printf("%d\n",fun1(14837));
}
int fun1(int m)
{
return ((m)? m%10+fun1(m/10):0); }


5. void main()
{ printf("%d\n",fun(3,8)); }
int fun(int x, int y)
{
if(x>y)
return 1000;
return x+fun(x+1,y);
}
```

6. What function does recursion provide in a programme?

7. Describe how stack is used in recursion.

8. Explain the winding and unwinding phases.

9. Give an example and describe how to create a recursive function.

10. Give an example and explain the distinction between tail and non-tail recursion.

What is indirect recursion, exactly?

12. What distinguishes recursion from iteration?

13. Without keeping the data in an array, create a recursive function that accepts a line of text and displays it in reverse order.

14. Create a recursive function to count every prime number between p and q (inclusive) in this range.

15. When a positive integer m is divided by a positive integer n, create a recursive function to get the quotient.

16. Create a programme that uses recursive function to determine a number's binary equivalent.

17. Create a programme that reverses numbers using a recursive function.

18. To get the remaining when a positive integer m is divided by a positive integer n, write a programme using a recursive function.

19. Create a recursive function that shows a positive number in words, such as -four six five if the value is 465.

20. To print the pyramids, create a recursive function.

1 abcd

1 2 abc

1 2 3 ab

1 2 3 4 a

21. Write a recursive function to find the Binomial coefficient C(n,k), which is defined as:

C(n,0)=1

C(n,n)=1

C(n,k)=C(n-1,k-1)+C(n-1,k)

Chapter 18 STORAGE CLASSES

A variable must be fully defined by mentioning both its type and storage class. In other words, we can say that variables have "storage classes" in addition to a data type.

Because storage classes contain defaults, they have not yet been mentioned for any variable. When a variable is declared but its storage class is not specified, the compiler chooses a storage class based on the context in which the variable will be used. We can therefore state that each variable has a certain default storage class.

The name of the variable is used by the compiler to determine the precise location within the computer where the string of bits that indicate the values of the variable are stored.

Such a value can typically be found in memory or CPU registers, two different types of locations in a computer. Which of the aforementioned two locations a given variable's value is stored in depends on its storage class.

Recognising a variable's storage type depends on four characteristics.These include scope, life, default beginning value, and scope.

The following information about a variable is revealed by its storage class:

(i) The location of the variable's storage.

(ii) In the event that the variable's value is not given, what is its initial value?

(iii) What is the variable's scope? Which function or block is the variable available in.

(iv) How long a specific variable lasts (how long the variable is present in a programme).

In C, there are four types of storage: automatic, static, register, and external. For the aforementioned storage classes, the terms auto, static, registers, and exter are used, respectively.

When declaring a variable, we can also provide a storage class. Storage_class datatype variable_name is the basic grammar;

Properties

Automatic Storage Class

Syntax to declare automatic variable is:

auto datatype variablename;

Example:

auto int i;

Features of Automatic Storage Class are as follows

Storage: Memory

Default Initial Value: Garbage Value

Scope: Local to the block in which the variable is defined

Life: Long enough for the control to stay inside the block where the variable is defined.

Automatic variables are any variables that are declared inside a block or function without specifying the storage class. Therefore, every variable is an automated variable by default. Although we can specify automatic variables using the auto keyword, this is typically not done. Automatic variables can have the same name in different functions or blocks without a problem because they can only be known inside a function or block. Take a look at these next two operations:

void fun1() void fun1()

{ {

int x,y; auto int x,y;

/* Some statements*/ /*Some statements*/

} }

The declaration statements in the two functions mentioned above are equal since they both define x and y as automatic variables.

The function of automatic variables is seen in the programme below.

void test();

void main()

{

test(); test(); test();

}

void test()

{

auto int k=10; printf("%d\n",k); k++;

}

Output:

10

When the function test() is invoked in the programme above for the first time, the variable k is created and initialised to 10. K is destroyed once main() is called again. When the function test() is invoked a second time, k is created, initialised, and destroyed following the method's completion. Automatic variables were created as a result, and they were removed once the code had finished running.

Register Storage Class

Syntax to declare register variable is:

register datatype variablename;

Features of Register Storage Class are as follows:

Storage: CPU Registers

Default Initial Value: Garbage Value

Scope: Local to the block in which the variable is defined

Life: Long enough for the control to stay inside the block where the variable is defined

Only automatic variables can be used with the register storage class. Its range, lifespan, and starting value by default are identical to those of automated variables. The location of storage is the only distinction between register and automated variables. While register variables are kept in CPU registers, automatic variables are kept in memory. The processor contains registers, which are small storage devices. Variables kept in registers can be accessed significantly more quickly than register-held variables. In order to speed up programme execution, variables that are often utilised can be given the register storage class. Consider the declaration of loop counters as register variables, which are defined as follows:

```
int main()
{
register int a;
for(a=0;i<50000;i++)
printf("%d\t",a);
return 0;
}
```

Variable an is specified as a register variable since it served as a loop counter frequently in the programme mentioned above. Register merely asks the compiler to allot memory for the variable into the register; it is not a command. Memory will be allocated into the registers if there are free registers. Additionally, if no free registers are available, memory will only be allocated in RAM (acting as an automated variable as storage is in memory).

In CPU registers, any type of variable can be stored. If the microprocessor only has 16 bit registers, it is impossible for them to store float or double values, which need 4 and 8 bytes, respectively. However, the compiler will treat the float and double variables as belonging to the automatic storage class (i.e., will treat them like automatic variables) if you use the register storage class for a float or double variable.

Static Storage Class

Syntax to declare static variable is:

static datatype variablename;

Example:

static int i;

Features of Static Storage Class are as follows

Storage: Memory

Default Initial Value: Zero

Scope: Local to the block in which the variable is defined

Life: The variable's value persists during calls to different functions.

Check out the prior programme now that k has been declared static rather than automatic.

void test();

void main()

{

test();

test();

test();

}

void test()

```c
{
static int k=10;
printf("%d\n",k);
k++;
}
```

Output:

10

11

12

Because a variable is initialised only once when it is specified as static, the output of the aforementioned programme is 10, 11, and 12 in this case. Since the variable k is marked as static in this case, the value of k is initially set to 10, and when test() is called for the first time, it is increased by 1 to become 11. K is static, hence its value never changes. When test() is used a second time, k is still available with its previous value of 11, rather than being reinitialized to 10. Now that 11 has been printed, its value has been increased by 1 to equal 12. Similarly, the third time test() is called, 12(Old value) is written and its value changes to 13 when the command 'k++;' is run.

As a result, the primary distinction between automatic and static variables is that static variables are initialised to zero if not initialised while automatic variables, if not initialised, contain an unpredictable value (garbage value). Additionally, static variables do not disappear when the function is no longer active; rather, their value persists, so if the control returns to the same function again, the static variables will still have the values they did the first time.

The general recommendation is to avoid using static variables in programmes unless absolutely necessary since they take up memory space that could be utilised by other variables because their values remain stored in memory even when the variables are not being used.

External Storage Class

Syntax to declare static variable is:

extern datatype variablename;

Example:

extern int i;

Features of External Storage Class are as follows

Storage: Memory

Default Initial Value: Zero

Scope: Global

Life: As long as the program's execution doesn't end

In terms of scope, external variables are different from automatic, register, and static variables since they are global as opposed to local in automatic, register, and static variables. External variables are available to all functions that want to use them because they are defined outside of all functions.

The code may be split up into numerous files if the programme is particularly large, and then these files are compiled to create object codes. With the aid of a linker, these object codes were combined to produce a ".exe" file. If a global variable is used in one file during compilation but is declared in another, an undefined symbol error is produced. In order to avoid this, global variables and global functions must first be declared with the term extern before being used in any file. We will receive an undefined symbol error if the global variable is declared in the midst of the programme; thus, we must specify its prototype using the term extern.

Therefore, a variable can be specified as an external variable if it will be utilised in multiple functions and files. Uninitialized external variables have a value of 0. An external variable's type and name are declared in its declaration, and its storage is reserved in the definition, which also functions as a declaration. In the declaration but not the definition, the word extern is mentioned. Now consider the following four claims.

1. auto int a;

2. register int b;

3. static int c;

4. extern int d;

The last phrase is a declaration, whereas the previous three are definitions.

Let's say there are two files, File1.c and File2.c, respectively. They contain the following:

File1.c

```c
int n=10; void
hello()
{
printf("Hello
");
}
```

File2.c

```c
extern int n;
extern      void
hello();
void main()
{
printf("%d",  n);
hello();
}
```

The value of n in File2.c will be 10 in the programme File1.obj+ File2.obj=File2.exe.

Where to use which Storage Class for a particular variable:

In certain circumstances, we employ various storage classes in an effort to:

1. Reduce the amount of memory that the variables utilise.

2. Increase the program's execution speed.

The following guidelines specify which storage class should be executed at what time:

(a) If you want a variable's value to remain constant across calls to multiple functions, use the static storage class (optional).

(b) For speedier execution, employ the register storage class for variables that are used frequently in a programme. Loop counters are an example of a register storage class application.

(c) Only use the extern storage class for variables that are used by nearly all of the functions in a programme. This will prevent these variables from being passed as arguments when calling a function.

(d) Use the auto storage class if you don't need any of the aforementioned things.

Exercise:

[A] Answer the following Questions.

(a) What do you mean by a variable's storage class?

(b) Why is it necessary to register a storage class?

(c) What are the uses of each of C's storage classes, and how many of them are there?

(d) Why does a programme need static storage variables?

(e) If a variable's storage class is not specified in a programme, which storage class is considered the default storage class? Describe how it functions with a relevant example.

(f) Can a floating point variable be stored in CPU registers? If so, how?

(g) What do you mean by a variable's scope and life?

(h) Explain when and how to use each storage class.

(i) Describe what you mean by an external variable and the definition of it.

(j) What distinguishes auto variables from static variables in a programme?

(k) What do you mean by a variable's definition and declaration?

[B] What is the output of the following programs:

```
(a) void main()
{
static int a=6;
printf("\na=%d",a--);
if(a!=0)
main();
}
(b) void main()
{
int i,j;
for(i=1;i<5;i++)
{
```

```c
j=fun1(i);
printf("\n%d",j);
}
}
int fun1(int a) {
static int b=2;
int c=3;
b=a+b;
return(a+b+c);
}
(c) void main()
{
fun1();
fun1();
}
void fun1()
{
auto int x=0;
register int y=0;
static int z=0;
x++;
y++;
z++;
printf("\n%d%d%d",x,y,z);
}
(d) int a=10; void main()
{
int a=20;
{
int a=30; printf("%d\n",a);
```

}
printf("%d",a);
}

[C] State whether the following statements are True or False:

(a) The variables of the register storage class are unable to store float values.

(b) A class variable for automatic storage retains its value across calls to different functions.

(c) The register storage class variables are considered as static storage class variables if the CPU registers are not accessible.

(d) The automated variable's default value is zero.

(e) The extern keyword must be used in the declaration of a global variable if it is to be defined.

(f) The compiler will flash an error notice if we attempt to utilise the register storage class for a float variable.

(g) Every time control enters the block containing the variable, space for the variable's register storage class is allocated.

(h) Unless the variable is explicitly declared in the aforementioned functions, an extern storage class variable is not accessible to the functions that come before its definition.

(i) A static variable exists as long as the control is present in the block where it was defined.

(j) It is impossible to obtain a register variable's address.

[D] Following program calculates the sum of digits of the number 25634. Go through it and find out why is it necessary to declare the storage class of the variable sum as static.

```c
#include<stdio.h>
void main()
{ int m;
m=sumdigit(25634);
printf("\n%d",m);
}
int sumdigit(int n)
{
static int sum;
int p,q;
```

```c
p=n%10;
q=(n-p)/10;
sum=sum+p;
if(q!=0) sumdigit(q);
else
return(sum);
}
```

CHAPTER 19 ARRAYS

Introduction:

A data structure is the manner that data is kept in a computer and the functions that are used to retrieve it. A grouping of similar data items is a simple approach to conceptualise a data structure. A collection of variables of one kind that can be accessed using a common name makes up an array, which is a form of data structure. Each element of an array has a unique access number, or index, that can be used to access that element. It addresses the issue of manipulating and storing a lot of values.

Arrays:

Previously, we stored the values using variables. We must declare the variable and initialise it, which means giving it a value, before we can use it. If there are 1000 variables, declaring and initialising each one as well as managing 1000 variables is a time-consuming procedure. We employ the idea of an array to resolve this issue. Values of the same kind are stored in an array. A collection of memory locations known as an array are connected by the fact that they share the same name and type. We supply the array's name and the element's position number to refer to a specific location or element in the array.

One Dimensional Array

Declaration:

The array needs to be declared before it can be used in the programme.

Formula:

data_type array_name[size];

data_type denotes the type of the array's elements. array_name is a representation of the array name.

The array's size indicates how many elements can be kept there.

Example:

char grade[20], float sal[15], int age[100] Age is an array of integers in this case, and it can hold 100 pieces of the same type. The floating type array sal, which has a capacity of 15, can hold float values. A character type array called "grade" can hold 20 characters.

Initialization:

We can explicitly initialize arrays at the time of declaration.

Syntax:

```
data_type array_name[size]={value1, value2,.........valueN};
```

Initializers, also known as constant values, are assigned one by one to the array elements as follows: value1, value2, valueN.

Example:

```
marks[5] = 10, 2, 0, 23 4,
```

Following this setup, the array's elements have the following values: marks[0]=10, marks[1]=2, marks[2]=0, marks[3]=23, and marks[4]=4.

NOTE:

1. Specifying the array size in 1-D arrays is optional. The compiler thinks that the array's size is equal to the number of initializers if size is not specified during initialization.

Example:

```
int markings[]=10,2,0,23,4;
```

The size of the array marks is set to 5 in this instance.

2. Simply assigning an element from one array to another array does not duplicate it.

Example:

```
int a[5]={9,8,7,6,5};
int b[5];
b=a; //not valid
```

we have to copy all the elements by using for loop. for(a=i; i<5; i++)

```
b[i]=a[i];
```

Processing:

The for loop is mostly used for array processing. The total number of passes is equal to the number of elements in the array, and each pass processes one element.

Example: #include<stdio.h>

```
main()
{
int a[3],i;
for(i=0;i<=2;i++) //Reading the array values
{
```

```c
printf("enter the elements"); scanf("%d",&a[i]);
}
for(i=0;i<=2;i++) //display the array values
{
printf("%d",a[i]); printf("\n");
}
}
```

Three integer-type elements are read by and shown by this programme. Example: A C programme to print the array when each element has been increased by one.

```c
#include <stdio.h> void main()
{
int i;
int array[4] = {10, 20, 30, 40};
for (i = 0; i < 4; i++)
arr[i]++;
for (i = 0; i < 4; i++)
printf("%d\t", array[i]);
}
```

Example: 2

C Program to Print the Alternate Elements in an Array

```c
#include <stdio.h>
void main()
{
int array[10]; int i, j, temp;
printf("enter the element of an array \n"); for (i = 0; i < 10; i++)
scanf("%d", &array[i]);
printf("Alternate elements of a given array \n"); for (i = 0; i < 10; i += 2)
printf( "%d\n", array[i]) ;
```

Example-3

C program to accept N numbers and arrange them in an ascending order

```c
#include <stdio.h> void main()
{
int i, j, a, n, number[30]; printf("Enter the value of N \n"); scanf("%d", &n);
printf("Enter the numbers \n"); for (i = 0; i < n; ++i)
scanf("%d", &number[i]);
for (i = 0; i < n; ++i)
{
for (j = i + 1; j < n; ++j)
{
if (number[i] > number[j])
{
a =number[i];
number[i] = number[j];
number[j] = a;
}
}
}
printf("The numbers arranged in ascending order are given below \n"); for (i = 0; i < n; ++i)
printf("%d\n", number[i]);
}
```

Chapter 20 : TWO DIMENSIONAL ARRAYS

Up until now, we have only thought about one-dimensional arrays, or lines of elements. A two-dimensional array is necessary when the data is presented naturally in the form of a table, such as in a spreadsheet.

Declaration:

The syntax is same as for 1-D array but here 2 subscripts are used.

Syntax:

data_type array_name[rowsize][columnsize];

Rowsize specifies the no.of rows Columnsize specifies the no.of columns.

Example:

int a[4][5];

There are 4 rows and 5 columns in this 2-D array. Here, the array's initial and last components are a[0][0] and a[3][4], respectively, making a total of 4*5=20 elements.

col 0 col 1 col 2 col 3 col 4

row 0 a[0][0] a[0][1] a[0][2] a[0][3] a[0][4] row 1 a[1][0] a[1][1] a[1][2] a[1][3] a[1][4] row 2 a[2][0] a[2][1] a[2][2] a[2][3] a[2][4] row 3 a[3][0] a[3][1] a[3][2] a[3][3] a[3][4]

Initialization:

2-D arrays can be initialized in a way similar to 1-D arrays.

Example:

int m[4][3]={1,2,3,4,5,6,7,8,9,10,11,12};

The values are assigned as follows:

m[0][0]:1 m[0][1]:2 m[0][2]:3

m[1][0]:4 m[1][1]:5 m[3][2]:6 m[2][0]:7 m[2][1]:8 m[3][2]:9 m[3][0]:10 m[3][1]:11 m[3][2]:12

The initialization of group of elements as follows:

int m[4][3]={{11},{12,13},{14,15,16},{17}};

The values are assigned as:

m[0][0]:1 1 m[0][1]:0 m[0][2]:0 m[1][0]:12 m[1][1]:13 m[3][2]:0

m[2][0]:14 m[2][1]:15 m[3][2]:16 m[3][0]:17 m[3][1]:0 m[3][2]:0

Note:

The first dimension in 2-D arrays is optional, while the second dimension must always be present.

Example: int m[][3]={

{1,10},

{2,20,200},

{3},

{4,40,400} };

Since there are 4 roes in the initialization list, the first dimension in this case is 4. Matrix refers to a 2-D array.

Processing:

Two nested for loops are required to parse 2-D arrays. The inner loop shows the columns, while the outer loop shows the rows.

Example:

int a[4][5];

a) Reading values in a for(i=0;i<4;i++)

for(j=0;j<5;j++)

scanf("%d",&a[i][j]);

b) Displaying values of a for(i=0;i<4;i++)

for(j=0;j<5;j++)

printf("%d",a[i][j]);

Example 1:

Write a C program to find sum of two matrices

#include <stdio.h> #include<conio.h>

void main()

{

float a[2][2], b[2][2], c[2][2];

int i,j;

clrscr();

printf("Enter the elements of 1st matrix\n");

/* Reading two dimensional Array with the help of two for loop. If there is an array of 'n' dimension, 'n' numbers of loops are needed for inserting data to array.*/

```c
for(i=0;i<2;I++)
for(j=0;j<2;j++)
{
scanf("%f",&a[i][j]);
}
printf("Enter the elements of 2nd matrix\n");
for(i=0;i<2;i++)
for(j=0;j<2;j++)
{
scanf("%f",&b[i][j]);
}
/* accessing corresponding elements of two arrays. */ for(i=0;i<2;i++)
for(j=0;j<2;j++)
{
c[i][j]=a[i][j]+b[i][j]; /* Sum of corresponding elements of two arrays. */
}
/* To display matrix sum in order. */ printf("\nSum Of Matrix:"); for(i=0;i<2;++i)
{
for(j=0;j<2;++j)
printf("%f", c[i][j]);
printf("\n");
}
getch();
}
```

Example 2: Program for multiplication of two matrices

```c
#include<stdio.h> #include<conio.h> int main()
{ int i,j,k;
int row1,col1,row2,col2,row3,col3;
int mat1[5][5], mat2[5][5], mat3[5][5];
clrscr();
```

```c
printf("\n enter the number of rows in the first matrix:");
scanf("%d", &row1);
printf("\n enter the number of columns in the first matrix:");
scanf("%d", &col1);
printf("\n enter the number of rows in the second matrix:");
scanf("%d", &row2);
printf("\n enter the number of columns in the second matrix:");
scanf("%d", &col2);
if(col1 != row2)
{
printf("\n The number of columns in the first matrix must be equal to the number of rows in the second matrix ");
getch(); exit();
}
row3= row1; col3= col3;
printf("\n Enter the elements of the first matrix");
for(i=0;i<row1;i++)
{
for(j=0;j<col1;j++)
scanf("%d",&mat1[i][j]);
}
printf("\n Enter the elements of the second matrix");
for(i=0;i<row2;i++)
{
for(j=0;j<col2;j++)
scanf("%d",&mat2[i][j]);
}
for(i=0;i<row3;i++)
{
for(j=0;j<col3;j++)
```

```c
{
mat3[i][j]=0;
for(k=0;k<col3;k++)
mat3[i][j] +=mat1[i][k]*mat2[k][j];
}
}
printf("\n The elements of the product matrix are"):
for(i=0;i<row3;i++)
{
printf("\n");
for(j=0;j<col3;j++)
printf("\t %d", mat3[i][j]);
}
return 0;
}
```

Output:

Enter the number of rows in the first matrix: 2

Enter the number of columns in the first matrix: 2

Enter the number of rows in the second matrix: 2

Enter the number of columns in the second matrix: 2

Enter the elements of the first matrix

1 2 3 4

Enter the elements of the second matrix

5 6 7 8

The elements of the product matrix are

19 22

43 50

Example 3:

Program to find transpose of a matrix.

```c
#include <stdio.h>
```

```c
int main()
{
int a[10][10], trans[10][10], r, c, i, j;
printf("Enter rows and column of matrix: ");
scanf("%d %d", &r, &c);
printf("\nEnter elements of matrix:\n");
for(i=0; i<r; i++)
for(j=0; j<c; j++)
{
printf("Enter elements a%d%d: ",i+1,j+1);
scanf("%d", &a[i][j]);
}
/* Displaying the matrix a[][] */ printf("\n Entered Matrix: \n"); for(i=0; i<r; i++)
for(j=0; j<c; j++)
{
printf("%d ",a[i][j]);
if(j==c-1)
printf("\n\n");
}
/* Finding transpose of matrix a[][] and storing it in array trans[][]. */ for(i=0; i<r;i++)
for(j=0; j<c; j++)
{
trans[j][i]=a[i][j];
}
/* Displaying the array trans[][]. */ printf("\nTranspose of Matrix:\n"); for(i=0; i<c;i++)
for(j=0; j<r;j++)
{
printf("%d ",trans[i][j]);
if(j==r-1)
printf("\n\n");
```

} return 0;

}

Output

Enter the rows and columns of matrix: 2 3

Enter the elements of matrix:

Enter elements a11: 1

Enter elements a12: 2

Enter elements a13: 9

Enter elements a21: 0

Enter elements a22: 4

Enter elements a23: 7

Entered matrix:

1 2 9

0 4 7

Transpose of matrix:

1 0

2 4

9 7

Multidimensional Array

Multidimensional arrays are those with more than two dimensions.

Example:

int a[2][3][4];

Here, a stands for two 2-dimensional arrays, each of which has three rows and four columns.

The individual elements are:

a[0][0][0],a[0][0][1],a[0][0][2],a[0][1][0]…………a[0][3][2]

a[1][0][0],a[1][0][1],a[1][0][2],a[1][1][0]…………..a[1][3][2]

the total no. of elements in the above array is 2*3*4=24.

Initialization:

int a[2][4][3]={

{

{1,2,3},

{4,5},

{6,7,8},

{9}

},

{

{10,11},

{12,13,14},

{15,16},

{17,18,19}

}

}

The values of elements after this initialization are as:

a[0][0][0]:1 a[0][0][1]:2 a[0][0][2]:3 a[0][1][0]:4 a[0][1][1]:5 a[0][1][2]:0

a[0][2][0]:6 a[0][2][1]:7 a[0][2][2]:8

a[0][3][0]:9 a[0][3][1]:0 a[0][3][2]:0

a[1][0][0]:10 a[1][0][1]:11 a[1][0][2]:0 a[1][1][0]:12 a[1][1][1]:13 a[1][1][2]:14 a[1][2][0]:15

a[1][2][1]:16 a[1][2][2]:0 a[1][3][0]:17 a[1][3][1]:18 a[1][3][2]:19

Note: The last subscript varies most frequently and the first subscript fluctuates least frequently when multidimensional arrays are initialised.

Example:

```
#include<stdio.h>
main()
{
int d[5]; int i;
for(i=0;i<5;i++)
{
d[i]=i;
}
for(i=0;i<5;i++)
```

{
printf("value in array %d\n",a[i]);
}
}

pictorial representation of d will look like

d[0]	d[1]	1	2	3	4
d[2]	d[3]				
d[4]	0				

CHAPTER 21 ARRAYS USING FUNCTIONS

1-d arrays using functions

Passing individual array elements to a function

Individual array members can be passed as arguments to a function just like other straightforward variables.

Example:

```
#include<stdio.h> void check(int); void main()
{
int a[10],I;
clrscr();
printf("\n enter the array elements:"); for(i=0;i<10;i++)
{
scanf("%d",&a[i]);
check(a[i]);
}
void check(int num)
{
if(num%2==0)
printf("%d is even\n",num); else
printf("%d is odd\n",num);
}
```

Output:

enter the array elements:

1 2 3 4 5 6 7 8 9 10

1 is odd

2 is even

3 is odd

4 is even

5 is odd

6 is even

7 is odd

8 is even

9 is odd

10 is even

Example:

C program to pass a single element of an array to function

```c
#include <stdio.h>
void display(int a)
{
printf("%d",a);
}
int main()
{
int c[]={2,3,4};
display(c[2]); //Passing array element c[2] only.
Return 0;
}
```

Output

2 3 4

Passing whole 1-D array to a function

The formal arguments should be declared as an array variable of the same type. We can pass a whole array as an actual argument to a function.

Example:

```c
#include<stdio.h>
main()
{
```

```c
int I, a[6]={1,2,3,4,5,6};
func(a);
printf("contents of array:"); for(i=0;i<6;i++)
printf("%d",a[i]);
printf("\n");
}
func(int val[])
{
int sum=0,I;
for(i=0;i<6;i++)
{
val[i]=val[i]*val[i];
sum+=val[i];
}
printf("the sum of squares:%d", sum);
}
```

Output

contents of array: 1 2 3 4 5 6 the sum of squares: 91

Example.2:

To pass an array containing a person's age to a function, create a C programme. The average age should be determined by this function and displayed in the primary section.

```c
#include <stdio.h>
float average(float a[]);
int main()
{
float avg, c[]={23.4, 55, 22.6, 3, 40.5, 18};
avg=averageI; /* Only name of array is passed as argument. */
printf("Average age=%.2f",avg);
return 0;
}
```

```c
float average(float a[])
{
int I;
float avg, sum=0.0;
for(i=0;i<6;++i)
{
sum+=a[i];
}
avg =(sum/6);
return avg;
}
```
Output

Average age= 27.08

Solved Example:

22. Create a programme to locate the greatest n-bit value in an array.

```c
#include <stdio.h>
#include<conio.h>
void main()
{
int array[100], maximum, size, c, location = 1; clrscr();
printf("Enter the number of elements in array\n");
scanf("%d", &size);
printf("Enter %d integers\n", size);
for (c = 0; c < size; c++)
scanf("%d", &array[c]);
maximum = array[0];
for (c = 1; c < size; c++)
{
if (array[c] > maximum)
```

```c
{
maximum = array[c];
location = c+1;
}
}
printf("Maximum element is present at location %d and it's value is %d.\n", location, maximum);
getch();
}
```

Output:

Enter the number of elements in array

5

Enter 5 integers

2

4

7

9

1

Maximum element is present at location 4 and it's value is 9

2. Create a programme to enter an n-digit number. These digits can be used to create a number.

```c
# include<stdio.h> #include<conio.h> #include<math.h>
void main()
{
int number=0,digit[10], numofdigits,I; clrscr();
printf("\n Enter the number of digits:"); scanf("%d", &numofdigits); for(i=0;i<numofdigits;i++)
{
printf("\n Enter the %d th digit:", i);
scanf("%d",&digit[i]);
} i=0;
while(i<numofdigits)
{
```

```c
number= number + digit[i]* pow(10,i)
i++;
}
printf("\n The number is : %d",number);
getch();
}
```

Output:

Enter the number of digits: 3

Enter the 0th digit: 5

Enter the 1th digit: 4

Enter the 2th digit: 3

The number is: 543

3. Matrix addition:

```c
#include <stdio.h>
#include<conio.h>
void main() {
int m, n, c, d, first[10][10], second[10][10], sum[10][10]; clrscr();
printf("Enter the number of rows and columns of matrix\n");
scanf("%d%d", &m, &n);
printf("Enter the elements of first matrix\n");
for ( c = 0 ; c < m ; c++ ) for ( d = 0 ; d < n ; d++ )
scanf("%d", &first[c][d]);
printf("Enter the elements of second matrix\n");
for ( c = 0 ; c < m ; c++ ) for ( d = 0 ; d < n ; d++ )
scanf("%d", &second[c][d]);
for ( c = 0 ; c < m ; c++ )
for ( d = 0 ; d < n ; d++ )
sum[c][d] = first[c][d] + second[c][d];
printf("Sum of entered matrices:-\n");
for ( c = 0 ; c < m ; c++ )
```

```c
{
for ( d = 0 ; d < n ; d++ )
printf("%d\t", sum[c][d]);
printf("\n");
}
getch();
}
```

Output:

Enter the number of rows and columns of matrix

2

2

Enter the elements of first matrix

1 2

3 4

Enter the elements of second matrix

5 6

2 1

Sum of entered matrices:- 6 8

5 5

Exercise

1. Can a programme compute the sum of an array's elements?

2. Create a programme that prints a histogram using an array?

3. Create a dice-rolling programme 138tilizing an array rather than a switch?

4. Using bubble sort to order an array?

5. Create a binary search programme using an array.

6. Create a programme that switches the array's biggest and smallest numbers.

7. Create a programme to fill a square matrix with the values 0, 1, and -1 on the upper right triangle and the diagonals.

8. Create a programme to read a 2x2x2 array and display it.

9. Create a programme to determine how many elements in the array are duplicates.

10. Determine the average, variance, and standard deviation of an array of integers by computing their sum and values.

11. Create a programme that scans a matrix and sums the items above the primary diagonal.

12. Create a programme to calculate XA + YB where X=2, and Y=3 and A and B are matrices.

CHAPTER 22 STRINGS

A string is a collection of characters that are handled as one entity. A string can contain letters, numbers, and a number of special characters like +, -, *, /, and $. In C, string literals and string constants are denoted by double quotation marks like in the example below:

"1000 Main Street" (a street address)

"(080)329-7082" (a telephone number)

"Kalamazoo, New York" (a city)

In the C programming language, strings are kept in an array of the char type with the null character '0' at the end.

In order to account for the '0' null termination character, we must increase the size of the string array by one.

Syntax:

char fname[4];

The above statement declares a string with a maximum length of three characters, called fname. It can also be indexed in the same way as a typical array.

character	t	w	o	\0
ASCII code	116	119	41	0

Generalized syntax is:-

char str[size];

The string may be declared in this fashion since the last character would be the null character, allowing us to put size-1 characters in the array. For instance,

char mesg[10]; can store maximum of 9 characters.

We can use this method to print a string from a variable, like the four name string from earlier.

e.g., printf("First name:%s",fname);

More than one variable can be inserted. Conversion guidelines %s is used to insert a string, after which we print each %s of the string.

An array of characters makes up a string. It can therefore be indexed like an array.

char ourstr[6] = "EED";

– ourstr[0] is 'E'

– ourstr[1] is 'E'

– ourstr[2] is 'D'

– ourstr[3] is '\0'

– ourstr[4] is '\0' – ourstr[5] is '\0'

'E'	'E'	'D'	\0	'\0'	'\0'

Reading strings:

If we declare a string by writing char str[100];

then str can be read from the user by using three ways;

1. Using scanf() function

2. Using gets() function

3. Using getchar(), getch(), or getche() function repeatedly

By writing scanf("%s",str"), the string can be read using the scanf() function.

The biggest drawback of the scanf() function is that it quits as soon as it encounters a blank space, despite the fact that its syntax is well-known and simple to use. For instance, str will only include Hello if the user types Hello World. This is due to the scanf() function's termination of the string at the first instance of a blank space.

Example:

char str[10];

printf("Enter a string\n");

scanf("%s",str);

The gets() function is the next technique for reading a string. Writing will read the string.

gets(str);

The limitations of scanf() are overcome by the method gets(). The initial address of the string that will contain the input is passed to the gets() function. The gets() function automatically ends the string that was entered with the null character.

Example:

char str[10];

printf("Enter a string\n");

gets(str);

If an ending character is not encountered, the string can alternatively be read by continuously executing getchar() to read a series of single characters while simultaneously storing it in a character array as follows:

```
int i=0;
char str[10],ch;
getchar(ch);
while(ch!='\0')
{
str[i]=ch; // store the read character in str
i++;
getch(ch); // get another character
}
str[i]='\0'; // terminate str with null character
```

Writing string

The string can be displayed on screen using three ways:

1. Using printf() function

2. Using puts() function

3. Using putchar() function repeatedly

Pintf() may be used to display the string by writing printf("%s",str); We can also specify the width and precision in addition to %s. The precision provides the maximum number of characters to be displayed, while the width specifies the minimum output field width. Example:

printf("%5.3s",str);

In a field with a total of five characters, this statement would only print the first three; these three characters would also be right justified within the available width.

The puts() function is the following way to write a string. You may see the string by writing:

puts(str);

It uses the newline character ('n') to end the line. If there is a mistake, it produces an EOF(-1); otherwise, it returns a positive number.

The string can then be created by repeatedly executing the putchar() function to output a series of single characters.

```c
int i=0;
char str[10];
while(str[i]!='\0')
{
putchar(str[i]); // print the character on the screen
i++;
}
```

Example: Read and display a string

```c
#include<stdio.h>
#include<conio.h>
void main()
{
char str[20];
clrscr();
printf("\n Enter a string:\n"); gets(str);
scanf("The string is:\n"); puts(str);
getch(); }
```

Output:

Enter a string: vssut burla

The string is: vssut burla

CHAPTER 23 : COMMON FUNCTIONS IN STRING

COMMON FUNCTIONS IN STRING

Type	Method	Description
char	strcpy(s1, s2)	Copy string
char	strcat(s1, s2)	Append string
int	strcmp(s1, s2)	Compare 2 strings
int	strlen(s)	Return string length
char	strchr(s, int c)	Find a character in string
char	strstr(s1, s2)	Find string s2 in string s1

strcpy():

One string can be copied onto another string using it. The second string's content gets copied over to the first string's content.

Syntax:

strcpy (string 1, string 2);

Example:

char mystr[10];

mystr = "Hello"; // Error! Illegal !!! Because we are assigning the value to mystr which is not possible in case of an string. We can only use "=" at declarations of C-String.

strcpy(mystr, "Hello");

It sets value of mystr equal to "Hello".

strcmp():

It is utilised to compare the two strings' contents. If there is a discrepancy, the difference in ASCII values between the first occurrence of two distinct characters will show up.

Syntax:

int strcmp(string 1, string 2);

Example:

char mystr_a[10] = "Hello";

char mystr_b[10] = "Goodbye";

– mystr_a == mystr_b; // NOT allowed! The correct way is

if (strcmp(mystr_a, mystr_b))

printf ("Strings are NOT the same.");

else

printf("Strings are the same.");

Here it will check the ASCII value of H and G i.e, 72 and 71 and return the diference 1.

strcat():

It is used to concatenate i.e, combine the content of two strings.

Syntax:

strcat(string 1, string 2);

Example:

char fname[30]={"bob"};

char lname[]={"by"};

printf("%s", strcat(fname,lname));

Output:

bobby.

strlen():

It is used to return the length of a string.

Syntax:

int strlen(string);

Example:

char fname[30]={"bob"}; int length=strlen(fname); It will return 3

strchr():

It is used to locate a character within the string and returns the position where the character appears for the first time.

Syntax:

strchr(cstr);

Example:

char mystr[] = "This is a simple string"; char pch = strchr(mystr,'s');

The output of pch is mystr[3]

strstr():

It is used to determine whether a string exists inside of another string and returns the string's initial starting index.

Syntax:

strstr(cstr1, cstr2);

Example:

Char mystr[]="This is a simple string"; char pch = strstr(mystr, "simple");

here pch will point to mystr[10]

• **String input/output library functions**

Function prototype	Function description
int getchar(void);	Inputs the next character from the standard input and returns it as integer
int putchar(int c);	Prints the character stored in c and returns it as an integer
int puts(char s);	Prints the string s followed by new line character. Returns a non-zero integer if possible or EOF if an error occurs
int sprint(char s, char format,....)	Equivalent to printf,except the output is stored in the array s instead of printed in the screen. Returns the no.of characters written to s, or EOF if an error occurs
int sprint(char s, char format,....)	Equivalent to scanf, except the input is read from the array s rather than from the keyboard. Returns the no.of items successfully read by the function , or EOF if an error occurs

NOTE:

Character arrays are known as strings.

Self-review exercises:

1. In each of the following programme portions, locate the issue and describe how to fix it:

• char s[10];

• strcpy(s,"hello",5);

• prinf("%s\n",s);

• printf("%s",'a');

• char s[12]; strcpy(s,"welcome home");

• If (strcmp(string 1, sring 2))

{ printf("the strings are equal\n");

}

2. A string of vowels is used to initialise a character array of vowels in two separate ways. "AEIOU"?

3. Create a programme that turns a string into an integer.

4. Create a programme that can receive a word and a line of text. Show the number of times that word appears in the text?

5. Create a programme that will read a word and rewrite its letters in the alphabet.

6. Create a programme that will insert a word into the text before a specific word.

7. Create a programme to count the characters, words, and lines in the text that is provided.

MODULE 3
CHAPTER 24 STRUCTURE AND UNION

Definition

A user-defined data type called a structure can be used to group together relevant pieces of information. Each variable in a structure has a name that may be used to choose it from the structure. These variables are of various data kinds. Structure is another user-defined data type that is accessible in C programming and lets you combine data items of different kinds. C arrays allow you to construct types of variables that can hold numerous data items of the same kind.

Records are represented by structures, Imagine you wish to manage the books you have in a library. You might want to keep track of each book's following characteristics:

• Title

• Author

• Subject

• Book ID

Structure Declaration

It is declared by using the term struct and the structure's name. The structure's variables are stated within the structure.

Example:

Struct struct-name

{

data_type var-name;

data_type var-name;

};

Structure Initialization

Initialising a structure is the process of assigning constants to its members.

Syntax:

struct struct_name

{

data _type member_name1;

data _type member_name2;

} struct_var={constant1,constant2};

Accessing the Members of a structure

Typically, the '.' operator is used to retrieve a structural member variable.

The dot operator is used to choose a specific structure member. Syntax: strcut_var. member_name.

putting a value on the person

We list the following data items for the structure variable stud: stud.roll=01; stud.name="Rahul";

You can enter values for the structure variable stud's data members by writing scanf("%d",&stud.roll");

scanf(''%s",&stud.name);

To print the values of structure variable stud, can be written as:

printf("%s",stud.roll);

printf("%f",stud.name);

QUESTIONS

1. To read and display the information about an employee, write a programme utilising structures.

2. Create a programme that can read, show, add, and take two complex integers out of each other.

3. Create a programme that allows users to enter two points and determine their distance from one another.

CHAPTER 25 NESTED STRUCTURES

A nested structure is a structure that has another structure as one of its components, or a structure inside of another structure. It is best to define each structure individually before grouping them into high-level structures.

1. Create a programme utilising nested structures to read and display the data of every student in the class.

Passing Structures through pointers

A variable that stores the address of a structure is called a pointer to a structure. The following syntax can be used to declare a pointer to a structure: strcut struct_name *ptr;

We would write ptr_stud=&stud; to assign the address of the stud to the pointer using the address operator (&).

The (->) operator is used to access the members of the structure.

for example

Ptr_stud->name=Raj;

SELF REFERENTIAL STRUCTURE

Structures that contain a reference to data of the same type as the structure are said to be self-referential.

Example

struct node

{

int val;

struct node*next;

};

Pointers to Structures

Similar to how you define a pointer to any other variable, you can define pointers to structures as follows:

struct books *struct_pointer;

The address of a structural variable can now be stored in the pointer variable that was previously defined. Place the & operator before the structure's name as shown below to determine the location of a structure variable:

struct_pointer = &book1;

Using a pointer to that structure, you must use the -> operator as shown below to access the members of that structure:

struct_pointer->title;

1. Write a programme that add, subtract, and show two times that are determined by the hour, minute, and second values.

2. Create a programme to initialise the structure's members using a pointer to the structure. Print the information about the pupils using functions.

3. Create a programme that reads and displays student data using an array of pointers to a structure.

CHAPTER 26 UNION

Information can only be kept in one field at a time in a union, which is a collection of variables with various data types. In C, there is a unique data type called a union that lets you store many data types in the same memory address. A union can have numerous members, but only one of those members can ever have a value present. Unions offer a practical method for serving many purposes with the same memory location.

Declaring Union

union union-name

{

data_type var-name;

data_type var-name;

};

Each member definition is a typical variable definition, such as int i, float f, or any other acceptable variable definition, and the union tag is optional. It is optional to specify one or more union variables before the last semicolon at the end of the union specification. This is how a union type called Data, which contains the three members i, f, and str, would be defined. Now, a Data type variable can hold a string of characters, a floating-point value, or an integer. This implies that different types of data can be stored in the same memory area using a single variable. Depending on your needs, you can utilise any built-in or user-defined data types inside a union.

A union will have enough space in its memory to accommodate its largest member. For instance, in the example above, the data type will take up 20 bytes of memory space because this is the maximum amount of space that a character string can use. The example that will show the total amount of memory that the aforementioned union has used is as follows:

Accessing a Member of a Union

#include <stdio.h> #include <string.h> union Data

{

int i;

float f;

char str[20];

```c
};
int main( )
{
union Data data;
data.i = 10;
data.f = 220.5;
strcpy( data.str, "C Programming");
printf( "data.i : %d\n", data.i);
printf( "data.f : %f\n", data.f);
printf( "data.str : %s\n", data.str); return 0;
}
```

To contact a union member, use the dot operator. The period that is coded between the name of the union variable and the union member that we want to access is the member access operator. To define variables of the union type, use the union keyword. Here's an illustration of how to use union:

Exercises:

1. Create a programme that defines a union and a structure with the exact identical members in both cases. Print the sizes of the structure and union variables using the sizeof operator, then explain the outcome.

2. Create a programme to establish a hotel structure with each member's name, address, grade, number of rooms, and room rates. Create a method to output the hotel names for a specific grade. Create a function that prints the names of hotels with room rates below the required amount as well.

CHAPTER 27 POINTERS

A variable that holds the address of a variable is called a pointer. Pointers are frequently used in C, in part because they are occasionally the only way to express a computation and in part because they typically produce more compact and efficient code than is possible using alternative methods. This chapter examines and demonstrates how to take use of the link between pointers and arrays. Pointers and the goto statement have been grouped together as a fantastic technique to write programmes that are tough to understand. This is undoubtedly the case when they are used carelessly, and pointers that point in unexpected directions are simple to make. But pointers can also be utilised to achieve clarity and simplicity if they are used with discipline. We shall attempt to illustrate this aspect.

The key modification to ANSI C is the clarification of the guidelines for manipulating pointers, thereby enforcing what good programmers already do and what excellent compilers already do. In addition, the appropriate type for a generic pointer has been changed from char * to void * (reference to void).

Pointers and Addresses

Let's start with a condensed representation of how memory is structured. A typical machine comprises a collection of memory cells with successive numbers or addresses that can be operated on individually or collectively. Any byte can function as a character, a pair of one-byte cells can be used to represent a short integer, and four adjacent bytes can be used to represent a long. A pointer is a collection of cells that can store an address (often two or four). We could therefore describe the scenario in the following manner if c is a char and p is a pointer that points to it:

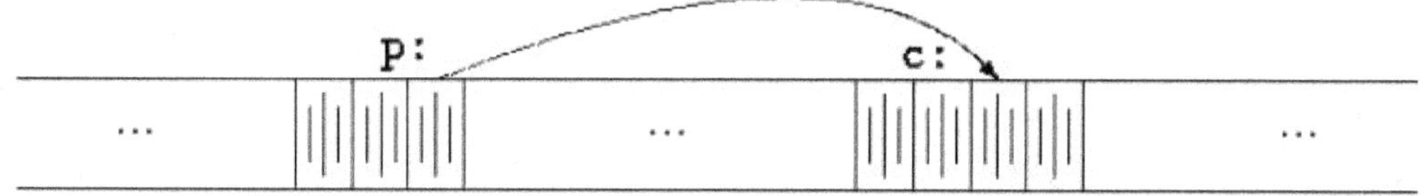

The unary operator &gives the address of an object, therefore the sentence p = &c; assigns the address of c to the variable p, and p is said to "point to" c. Only variables and array elements that are in memory are applicable to the &operator. Expressions, constants, and register variables are not subject to it.

When used with a pointer, the unary operator *, also known as the indirection or dereferencing operator, allows access to the object that the pointer refers to. Assume that ip is a reference to an int and that x and y are both integers. This fictitious sequence demonstrates the declaration of a pointer and the use of &and *:

int x = 1, y = 2, z[10];

int *ip;

ip = &x;

y = *ip;

*ip = 0;

ip = &z[0];

We have been watching the proclamation of x, y, and z the entire time. the IP pointer's declaration.

int *ip;

is a mnemonic that explains that the phrase *ipis an int. A variable's declaration replicates the syntax of any possible expressions in which it might appear. The same logic is true for function declarations. For instance,

double *dp, atof(char *);

claims that the values of the expressions *dp and atof(s) are double, and that the argument to atof is a pointer to a char.

The fact that every pointer links to a particular data type implies that a pointer is restricted to pointing to a certain sort of object. If the number ippoints to, then *ipcan occur in any situation where x could, so

*ip = *ip + 10;

increments *ip by 10.

Assignment is easier because the unary operators * and &bind more tightly than arithmetic operators.

y = *ip + 1

takes whatever ippoints at, adds 1, and assigns the result to y, while

*ip += 1

increments what ippoints to, as do

++*ip and (*ip)++

In this final example, brackets are required because, without them, unary operators like * and ++ associate right to left, which would lead the expression to increment ip rather than the value it points to. Pointers can also be utilised without dereferencing because they are variables. For instance, if iq is a different int pointer, iq = ip replicates what is in ipin into iq, making iqpoint to whatever is in ipin.

Pointers and Function Arguments

There is no direct mechanism for the called function to change a variable in the calling function since C delivers parameters to functions by value. For instance, a sorting algorithm might use the swap function to swap two out-of-order parameters. Writing is not sufficient.

swap(a, b);

where the swap function is defined as

void swap(int x, int y)

{

int temp;

temp = x;

x = y;

y = temp;

}

Swap cannot change the inputs a and b in the function that called it due to call by value. The a and b copies are switched in the function above. The caller programme must pass pointers to the values that need to be altered in order to achieve the desired result:

swap(&a, &b);

&a is a pointer to a because the operator & generates the address of a variable. The operands are accessed indirectly through the parameters, which are defined as pointers in the swap function itself.

void swap(int *px, int *py) /* interchange *px and *py */

{

int temp;

```c
temp = *px;

*px = *py;

*py = temp;

}
```

A function can access and modify items in the function that called it by using pointer parameters. Take the function getint, for instance, which converts free-format input by dividing a stream of characters into integer values, one integer per call. When there is no more input, getint must notify the end of the file and return the value it discovered. Since any value used for EOF could also be the value of an input integer, these values must be returned via different pathways.

One approach is to use a pointer argument to keep the converted integer back in the calling function while having getint return the end of file status as the function value. This is the method that scanfas use. well

By using getint calls, the following loop populates an array with integers:

```c
int n, array[SIZE], getint(int *);

for (n = 0; n < SIZE &&getint(&array[n]) != EOF; n++)

;
```

Each call increments n and sets array[n] to the following integer in the input. Keep in mind that you must supply getint with the address of array[n]. Without this, getint is unable to return the converted integer to the caller.

Our implementation of getintreturns EOF for end of file, zero if the following input does not contain a number, and a positive value if it does.

```c
#include <ctype.h>

int getch(void);

void ungetch(int);

int getint(int *pn)

{

int c, sign;

while (isspace(c = getch()));

if (!isdigit(c) && c != EOF && c != '+' && c != '-')

{
```

```c
ungetch(c); return 0;
}
sign = (c == '-') ? -1 : 1;
if (c == '+' || c == '-')
c = getch();
for (*pn = 0; isdigit(c), c = getch())
*pn = 10 * *pn + (c - '0');
*pn *= sign;
if (c != EOF)
ungetch(c);
return c;
}
```

*pnis utilised as an ordinary int variable throughout getint. In order to push the one additional character that needs to be read back onto the input, we have additionally used getchand ungetch.

```c
int x = 1, y = 2, z[10];
int *ip;
ip = &x;
y = *ip;
*ip = 0;
ip = &z[0];
```

We have been watching the proclamation of x, y, and z the entire time. the IP pointer's declaration. int *ip; is a mnemonic that explains that the phrase *ipis an int. A variable's declaration replicates the syntax of any possible expressions in which it might appear. The same logic is true for function declarations. For instance, double *dp, atof(char *); claims that the values of the expressions *dp and atof(s) are double, and that the argument to atof is a pointer to a char.

The fact that every pointer links to a particular data type implies that a pointer is restricted to pointing to a certain sort of object. If the number ippoints to, then *ipcan occur in any situation where x could, so

```c
*ip = *ip + 10;
```

increments *ip by 10.

Assignment is easier because the unary operators * and &bind more tightly than arithmetic operators.

y = *ip + 1

takes whatever ippoints at, adds 1, and assigns the result to y, while

*ip += 1

increments what ippoints to, as do

++*ip and (*ip)++

In this final example, brackets are required because, without them, unary operators like * and ++ associate right to left, which would lead the expression to increment ip rather than the value it points to. Pointers can also be utilised without dereferencing because they are variables. For instance, if iq is a different int pointer, iq = ip replicates what is in ipin into iq, making iqpoint to whatever is in ipin.

Pointers and Function Arguments

There is no direct mechanism for the called function to change a variable in the calling function since C delivers parameters to functions by value. For instance, a sorting algorithm might use the swap function to swap two out-of-order parameters. Writing is not sufficient.

swap(a, b);

where the swap function is defined as

void swap(int x, int y)

{

int temp;

temp = x;

x = y;

y = temp;

}

Swap cannot change the inputs a and b in the function that called it due to call by value. The a and b copies are switched in the function above. The caller programme must pass pointers to the values that need to be altered in order to achieve the desired result:

swap(&a, &b);

As the address of a variable is produced by the operator &, &a is a pointer to a. The operands are accessed indirectly through the swap function's parameters, which are defined as pointers.

```c
void swap(int *px, int *py) /* interchange *px and *py */
{
int temp;
temp = *px;
*px = *py;
*py = temp;
}
```

A function can access and modify items in the function that called it by using pointer parameters. Take the function getint, for instance, which converts free-format input by dividing a stream of characters into integer values, one integer per call. When there is no more input, getint must notify the end of the file and return the value it discovered. Since any value used for EOF could also be the value of an input integer, these values must be returned via different pathways.

One approach is to use a pointer argument to keep the converted integer back in the calling function while having getint return the end of file status as the function value. This is the method that scanfas use. well

By using getint calls, the following loop populates an array with integers:

```c
int n, array[SIZE], getint(int *);
for (n = 0; n < SIZE &&getint(&array[n]) != EOF; n++)
    ;
```

Each call increments n and sets array[n] to the following integer in the input. Keep in mind that you must supply getint with the address of array[n]. Without this, getint is unable to return the converted integer to the caller.

Our implementation of getintreturns EOF for end of file, zero if the following input does not contain a number, and a positive value if it does.

```c
#include <ctype.h>
int getch(void);
void ungetch(int);
int getint(int *pn)
```

```c
{
int c, sign;
while (isspace(c = getch()));
if (!isdigit(c) && c != EOF && c != '+' && c != '-')
{
ungetch(c); return 0;
}
sign = (c == '-') ? -1 : 1;
if (c == '+' || c == '-')
c = getch();
for (*pn = 0; isdigit(c), c = getch())
*pn = 10 * *pn + (c - '0');
*pn *= sign;
if (c != EOF)
ungetch(c);
return c;
}
```

*pnis utilised as an ordinary int variable throughout getint. In order to push the one additional character that needs to be read back onto the input, we have additionally used getchand ungetch.

CHAPTER 28 Pointers and Arrays

Pointers and arrays in the C programming language have a close link that calls for their discussion together. Pointers can be used to do every action that array subscripting can. The pointer version will typically be quicker but, at least to the layman, a little more difficult to comprehend. The statement int a[10]; designates a block of 10 consecutive objects with the names a[0], a[1],., and a[9] that make up an array of size 10. The i-th element of the array is indicated by the notation a[i]. The assignment pa = &a[0]; sets pa to point to element zero of a, i.e., pa contains the address of a[0], if pa is a pointer to an integer specified as int *pa. The task x =*pa; will now copy the data from a[0] into x.

If an array's element pa points to a specific one, then pa+1 points to the element after it, pa+i points to the element after pa, and pa-i points to the element before. As a result, if pa points to a[0], *(pa+1) denotes the information in a[1,] pa+iis the address of a[i], and *(pa+i) denotes the information in a[i]. These statements are accurate regardless of the kind or quantity of variables in array a.

All pointer arithmetic, including "adding 1 to a pointer," means that pa+1 points to the object after pa, and pa+i points to the i-th item after pa. Pointer arithmetic and indexing closely resemble one other. The address of array element zero is, by definition, the value of a variable or expression of type array. so following the assignment pa = &a[0]; Pa and an are equal in value. The assignment pa=&a[0] can also be written as pa = a since the name of an array is a synonym for the position of the first element.

At first glance, it may seem more unexpected that a reference to a[i] can alternatively be expressed as *(a+i). C immediately changes a[i] to *(a+i) after evaluating it; the two forms are identical. It follows that &a[i] and a+iare likewise equivalent when the operator &is applied to both sides of this equivalence because a+iis the address of the i-th element after a. The flip side of this is that expressions may use pa with a subscript if it is a pointer; pa[i] is equivalent to *(pa+i). In essence, an expression expressed as a pointer and offset is equivalent to one written as an array and index. A pointer and an array name differ in one important way that must be remembered. Pa=a and pa++ are acceptable since a pointer is a type of variable. However, an array name is not a variable, hence it is forbidden to use expressions like a=pa and a++.

The location of the first element is supplied when an array name is passed to a function. This argument is a local variable inside the called function, making an array name parameter a pointer— a variable with an address. This information allows us to create a different iteration of the string length calculator, strlen.

```
int strlen(char *s)
{
int n;
for (n = 0; *s != '\0', s++)
n++;
return n;
}
```

Since s is a pointer, increasing it is totally acceptable; s++ simply increases strlen's private copy of the pointer and has no impact on the character string in the function that called strlen. Thus, strlen("hello, world"), strlen(array), and strlen(ptr) all function as expected.

Both char s[]; and char *s; are equivalent as formal parameters in a function specification, but we prefer the latter since it makes the variable's status as a pointer more clear. When a function receives the name of an array, the function may, at its discretion, interpret the name as either an array or a pointer and act accordingly. In cases where it seems suitable and straightforward, it may even employ both notations.

A pointer to the start of the subarray can be used to pass a portion of an array to a function. For instance, if an is an array, f(&a[2]) and f(a+2) both send the address of the subarray that begins at a[2] to the function f. The argument declaration within f can be written as f(intarr[]) ... or f(int *arr) ...

Therefore, it makes no difference to f that the parameter relates to a subset of a bigger array.

It is also feasible to index backwards in an array if one is certain that the items exist; p[-1], p[-2], and so on are syntactically acceptable and refer to the elements that come just after p[0]. Of course, referring to items outside of the array bound is prohibited.

CHAPTER 29 Pointer Arithmetic

If p points to an element in an array, p++ advances it to point to the next element, and p+=i advances it to point elements further than it does now. The simplest types of pointer or address arithmetic are those that use this and comparable constructs. With pointers, not all arithmetic operations are possible. The legitimate activities that pointers are capable of doing are

(i) The increment and addition of an integer to a pointer.

(ii) An integer is subtracted from a pointer and a decrement operation is performed.

(iii) A pointer is subtracted from another pointer of the same type.

The following arithmetic operations cannot be carried out on pointers:

(i) Multiplication, division, and addition of two pointers.

(ii) Multiplication of any number by the pointer.

(iii) Division by any number of a pointer.

(iv) Pointers can have float or double values added to them.

The correct machine address for the subsequent variable of that type is produced by the equation p+1. other acceptable pointer expressions

p+i, ++p, p+=I, p-q

where the number of array entries between p and q is represented by p-q.

A pointer can be added to in order to traverse an array because it is simply a mem address. P+1 gives a pointer to the following array element.

The * operator has the same amount of precedence as the increment/decrement operators, and they are associative from right to left. In actuality, p+1 increases the memory address by the size of the array element, not by 1.

Assume that x is an integer variable and that p is an integer pointer. The primary challenge now is to determine how the following pointer expressions shown below are to be understood.

(i) x = *p++ is same as two expressions x = *p followed by p = p + 1.

(ii) x = (*p)++ is same as two expressions x = *p followed by *p = *p + 1.

(iii) x=*++p is same as two expressions p=p+1 followed by x=*p.

(iv) x=++*p is same as two expressions *p=*p+1 followed by x=*p

One of the benefits of the language is how pointers, arrays, and address arithmetic are integrated. C is consistent and regular in its approach to address arithmetic. Let's use the creation of a simple storage allocator as an example. Two routines exist. The first, alloc(n), provides the caller with a pointer to n consecutive character locations that can be used to store characters. The second, afree(p), releases the storage that was so gained so that it may be utilised again in the future.

The "rudimentary" nature of the routines is due to the requirement that the calls to afree be made in the reverse order of the calls to alloc. In other words, the storage that allocand afree manages is a stack, or last-in, first-out storage. Similar functions called malloc and free from the standard library are available and do not have these limitations.

The simplest method is to allochand out portions of an enormous character array, which we shall refer to as allocbuf. This array has been set aside for exclusive use. No other function needs to know the name of the array because it can be declared static in the source file containing allocand afree and hence be invisible outside of it because they deal in pointers rather than array indices. The array might not even have a name in practical implementations; instead, it might be obtained by executing mallocor and asking the operating system for a pointer to an unnamed storage block. How much of the allocbuf has been used is the other piece of information required. We employ a pointer called allocp that directs attention to the following free element. When allocis requests n characters, it determines whether there is still space in allocbuf. In this case, allocre increments the value of allocp by n to point to the following free area after returning the current value of allocp (i.e., the start of the free block). In the absence of space, allocre yields 0. If p is present in allocbuf, afree(p) essentially sets allocpto p.

```c
#define ALLOCSIZE 10000 static char allocbuf[ALLOCSIZE];
static char *allocp = allocbuf; char *alloc(int n)
{
if (allocbuf + ALLOCSIZE - allocp>= n) { allocp += n;
return allocp - n;
} else return 0;
}
void afree(char *p)
{
```

```c
if (p >= allocbuf&& p <allocbuf + ALLOCSIZE) allocp = p;
}
```

Although often the only relevant values are zero or an expression involving the address of previously declared data of the right type, a pointer can be initialised in general just like any other variable. The character pointer allocp is defined to be a character pointer and initialised to point to the beginning of allocbuf, which is the next free location when the programme starts, by the statement static char *allocp = allocbuf;. Since the array name is the address of the zeroth element, static char *allocp = &allocbuf[0]; would have been a better alternative. If (allocbuf + ALLOCSIZE - allocp>= n) tests whether there is sufficient space to accommodate a request for n characters. The new value of allocpwould be at most one beyond the end of allocbuf if it were, though it is unlikely. Allocre returns a pointer to the first character in a block of characters if the request can be fulfilled (note the function's declaration). If not, alloc must return some indication that no more space is available. A return value of zero can be used to indicate an unexpected event, in this case no space, because C guarantees that zero is never a suitable address for data.

Integers and pointers cannot be used interchangeably. Zero is the only exception; a pointer may be compared to the constant zero and may have the constant zero allocated to it. As a mnemonic to make it easier to remember that this is a particular value for a pointer, the symbolic constant NULL is sometimes used in place of zero. In'stdio.h', NULL is defined. NULL will be used moving forward. Pointer arithmetic is demonstrated in numerous significant ways by tests like if (allocbuf + ALLOCSIZE - allocp>= n) and if (p >= allocbuf&& p allocbuf + ALLOCSIZE). First, under certain situations, pointers may be compared. Relations like ==,!=, and the like are applicable if p and q point to elements of the same array.

<, >=, etc., work properly. For example, p < q

is true if p points to an element in the array that is earlier than q. Any pointer's equality or inequality with zero can be meaningfully compared. For comparisons or calculations involving pointers that do not point to members of the same array, the behaviour is, nonetheless, undefinable. (There is one exception: pointer arithmetic can utilise the address of the first element past the end of an array.) Second, we've already seen that an integer and a pointer can be added to or removed from each other. The phrase "p + n" refers to the address of the n-th object after the one that "p" is now pointing to. No matter what kind of object p points to, this is true since n is scaled in accordance with the size of the objects p points to, which is defined by the declaration of p. For instance, if an int is four bytes, it will be scaled by four.

Pointer subtraction is also acceptable: q-p+1 is the number of items from p to q inclusive if p and q point to elements of the same array, and p q. This information can be utilised to create still another strlen variant:

```
int strlen(char *s)
{
char *p = s;
while (*p != '\0')
p++;
return p - s;
}
```

P is initialised to s, or the first character of the string, in its declaration. Each character is checked individually within the while loop until the final '0' is identified. Since p points to characters, p++ advances p each time to the following character, while p-s provides the number of characters advanced over, or the length of the string. (The string might include too many characters to fit in an int. The type ptrdiff_t is large enough to carry the signed difference of two pointer values and is defined in the header file stddef.h>. To match the standard library version, we would use size_t instead of strlen for the return result if we were being cautious. The sizeofoperator's unsigned integer type size_t is what it returns.

Since floats take up more storage space than chars, pointer arithmetic is consistent: if p were a pointer to a float, p++ would move on to the next float. Thus, by just changing char to float throughout allocand afree, we might create a different version of alloc that keeps floats rather than chars. The size of the objects being referred at is automatically taken into account in all pointer manipulations. Assignment of pointers of the same type, addition or subtraction of a pointer and an integer, comparison or subtraction of two pointers to elements of the same array, and assignment or comparison to zero are all acceptable pointer operations. All other pointer maths is forbidden. It is forbidden to assign a pointer of one type to a pointer of another type without a cast, with the exception of void *. It is also forbidden to multiply, divide, shift, mask, add float, or add double to two pointers.

CHAPTER 30 CHARACTER POINTERS AND FUNCTIONS

The phrase "I am a string" refers to a string constant, which is an array of characters. The array is ended with the null character "0" in the internal representation so that programmes can identify the end. As a result, the length in storage is one character longer than the characters between the double quotes.

String constants are frequently used as function arguments, for example, printf("hello, world");

A character pointer is used to retrieve a character string like this one when it comes in a programme; printf receives a pointer to the array's start. In other words, a pointer to a string constant's initial element is used to access it. Function parameters do not have to include string constants. The sentence pmessage = "now is the time"; assigns a pointer to the character array to pmessage if pmessage is specified as char *pmessage. There are only pointers involved; this is not a string copy. There are no operators in C that can handle a whole string of characters at once. Between these definitions, there is a significant distinction:

char amessage[] = "now is the time";

char *pmessage = "now is the time";

Amessage is an array that is only large enough to accommodate the character string and '0' used to initialise it. Although the array's individual letters are changeable, a message will always refer to the same storage. Pmessage, on the other hand, is a pointer that is initialised to refer to a constant string. You can change the pointer's location later, but if you try to change the text's contents, the outcome is undefined.

By examining modified versions of two practical functions taken from the standard library, we will show additional features of pointers and arrays. Strcpy(s,t) is the first function, and it copies the string t to the string s. While saying s=t would be good, doing so copies the pointer rather than the characters. We require a loop in order to replicate the characters. First, the array version

void strcpy(char *s, char *t)

{

inti;

i = 0;

while ((s[i] = t[i]) != '\0') i++; }

For contrast, here is a version of strcpywith pointers:

```c
void strcpy(char *s, char *t)
{
inti; i = 0;
while ((*s = *t) != '\0')
{ s++; t++; }
}
```

The parameters s and t can be used whenever strcpy sees fit because arguments are supplied by value. Here, they are provided with neatly initialised pointers that are marched down the arrays one character at a time until the '0' that ends t has been copied into s. Strcpy would not be written as we demonstrated above in real life. Experienced C programmers would prefer

```c
void strcpy(char *s, char *t)
{
while ((*s++ = *t++) != '\0')
;
}
```

As a result, the increment of s and t is moved into the loop's test section. The character that t originally pointed to before it was increased is the value of *t++; the postfix ++ doesn't modify t until this character has been fetched. The character is also stored into the former s place before s is increased in the same manner. In order to regulate the loop, this character's value is also compared to "0." Overall, characters up to and including the last "0" are copied from t to s.

The comparison against "0" in the final abbreviation is unnecessary because the only thing being asked is whether the expression is zero. The function would therefore probably be written as

```c
void strcpy(char *s, char *t)
{
while (*s++ = *t++)
;
}
```

Although this may initially appear confusing, the notational convenience is significant, and the phrase should be grasped since you will regularly encounter it in C programmes. The standard library's (string.h) strcpy function returns the target string as the value of its function. The second procedure we'll look at is strcmp(s,t), which compares the character strings s and t and returns true or false depending on whether s is lexicographically bigger or less than t. The value is calculated by removing the characters where s and t don't agree in the first place.

```
int strcmp(char *s, char *t)
{
inti;
for (i = 0; s[i] == t[i]; i++) if (s[i] == '\0')
return 0;
return s[i] - t[i];
}
```

The pointer version of strcmp:

```
int strcmp(char *s, char *t)
{
for ( ; *s == *t; s++, t++) if (*s == '\0')
return 0;
return *s - *t;
}
```

There are other, less common pairings of * and ++ and -- because ++ and -- are either prefix or postfix operators. For instance, before obtaining the character that p points to, *--p decreases p. The typical idiom for pushing and popping a stack is really the pair of expressions *p++ = val; val = *--p; The header string.h> provides declarations for the functions covered in this section as well as a number of other string-handling functions from the standard library.

Pointer Arrays; Pointers to Pointers

Datatype (*pointer_variable)[size] is the syntax to specify a pointer to an array; For instance, int (*ptr)[10];Here, ptr is a pointer that can point to an array of 10 integers. We can initialise ptr with the array's base address and then access different elements of the array by increasing ptr's value.

Pointers can be stored in arrays exactly like other variables because they are variables in and of themselves. As an example, let's create a streamlined version of the UNIX programme sort that would alphabetically arrange a set of text lines.

We require a data format that can easily and effectively handle text lines of different lengths. The array of pointers enters at this point. Each line can be accessed by a pointer to its initial character if the lines to be sorted are stored end to end in one lengthy character array. The actual pointers can be kept in an array. By providing the pointers of two lines to strcmp, two lines can be compared. The pointers in the pointer array are switched out instead of the actual text lines when two out-of-order lines need to be exchanged.

By doing this, the twin issues of difficult storage management and significant overhead associated with moving the lines themselves are avoided.

Three steps make up the sorting procedure:

read all the lines of input

sort them

print them in order

The programme should, as usual, be divided into functions that correspond to this natural division, with the main routine managing the other functions. Deferring the sorting process will allow us to focus on the data structure, input, and output for the time being. Each line's characters must be collected, saved, and an array of pointers to the lines must be created by the input routine. It will also need to count the number of input lines because sorting and printing depend on that data. Since the input function can only handle a limited number of input lines, it may return an illegal value, such as -1, if there is an excessive amount of input. Only the lines in the array of pointers' order must be printed by the output procedure.

```c
#include <stdio.h>
#include <string.h>
#define MAXLINES 5000
char *lineptr[MAXLINES];
intreadlines(char *lineptr[], intnlines);
void writelines(char *lineptr[], intnlines);
void qsort(char *lineptr[], int left, int right); main()
```

```c
{
intnlines;
if ((nlines = readlines(lineptr, MAXLINES)) >= 0) { qsort(lineptr, 0, nlines-1);
writelines(lineptr, nlines); return 0;
} else {
printf("error: input too big to sort\n");
return 1;
}
}
#define MAXLEN 1000
intgetline(char *, int);
char *alloc(int);
intreadlines(char *lineptr[], intmaxlines)
{
intlen, nlines;
char *p, line[MAXLEN];
nlines = 0;
while ((len = getline(line, MAXLEN)) > 0)
if (nlines>= maxlines || p = alloc(len) == NULL) return -1;
else {
line[len-1] = '\0'; /* delete newline */ strcpy(p, line);
lineptr[nlines++] = p;
}
return nlines;
}
void writelines(char *lineptr[], intnlines)
{
inti;
for (i = 0; i<nlines; i++) printf("%s\n", lineptr[i]);
}
```

The main new thing is the declaration for lineptr:

```
char *lineptr[MAXLINES]
```

lineptri is described as an array of MAXLINES items, each of which is a pointer to a char. In other words, *lineptr[i] is the character it points to, the first character of the i-th stored text line, and lineptr[i] is a character pointer.

Lineptri can be considered as a pointer in the same way as in our earlier instances as it is the name of an array itself, and writelines can be written as

```
void writelines(char *lineptr[], intnlines)
{
while (nlines-- > 0) printf("%s\n", *lineptr++);
}
```

*lineptr initially points to the first line; when nlines is counted down, each element moves it to the next line pointer.

We can go on to sorting after input and output are under control.

```
void qsort(char *v[], int left, int right)
{
inti, last;
void swap(char *v[], inti, int j);
if (left >= right) /* do nothing if array contains */ return; /* fewer than two elements */
swap(v, left, (left + right)/2);
last = left;
for (i = left+1; i<= right; i++) if (strcmp(v[i], v[left]) < 0) swap(v, ++last, i);
swap(v, left, last);
qsort(v, left, last-1);
qsort(v, last+1, right);
}
```

Similarly, the swap routine needs only trivial changes:

```
void swap(char *v[], inti, int j)
{
char *temp; temp = v[i];
```

v[i] = v[j]; v[j] = temp;

}

Since temp must be a character pointer in order for one to be transferred to the other, every element of v (also known as lineptr) must be one as well.

Multi-dimensional Arrays

Although C offers rectangular multi-dimensional arrays, pointer arrays are utilised much more frequently in practise. We shall demonstrate some of their characteristics in this section.

Take into account the issue of converting dates from a day of the month to a day of the year and vice versa. For instance, March 1 falls on a non-leap year's 60th day and a leap year's 61st day.

Let's construct two functions to perform the conversions: month_day translates the day of the year into the month and day, and day_of_year turns the month and day into the day of the year. Month and Day arguments for the latter function are pointers since it computes two values: month_day(1988, 60, &m, &d) sets m to 2 and d to 29 (February 29th).

Both of these services require the same data, a table with the number of days in each month (e.g., "September has thirty days," etc.). It is simpler to divide the months into two rows of a two-dimensional array than to keep track of what happens to February throughout calculation because the number of days in each month varies for leap years and non-leap years. The functions and array used for the transformations are as follows:

static char daytab[2][13] = {

{0, 31, 28, 31, 30, 31, 30, 31, 31, 30, 31, 30, 31},

{0, 31, 29, 31, 30, 31, 30, 31, 31, 30, 31, 30, 31}

};

intday_of_year(int year, int month, int day)

{

inti, leap;

leap = year%4 == 0 && year%100 != 0 || year%400 == 0; for (i = 1; i< month; i++)

day += daytab[leap][i];

return day;

}

void month_day(int year, intyearday, int *pmonth, int *pday)

```c
{
inti, leap;
leap = year%4 == 0 && year%100 != 0 || year%400 == 0; for (i = 1; yearday>daytab[leap][i]; i++)
yearday -= daytab[leap][i];
*pmonth = i;
*pday = yearday;
}
```

Remember that a logical expression, like the one for leap, can be used as a subscript of the array daytab since its arithmetic value is either zero (false) or one (true).

Both day_of_year and month_day can use the array daytab because it is external to both of those variables. We changed it to char to show how small non-character integers can be stored using char. The first two-dimensional array we dealt with was daytab. A two-dimensional array in C is actually a one-dimensional array with arrays as its elements. As a result, subscripts are written as daytab[i][j] instead of daytab[i,j].

A two-dimensional array can be processed in much the same way as in other languages, save from this notational difference. The rightmost subscript or column varies the quickest as elements are retrieved in storage order since elements are stored by rows.

A list of initializers enclosed in braces is used to initialise an array, and a corresponding sub-list is used to initialise each row of a two-dimensional array. Since month numbers naturally range from 1 to 12 rather than 0 to 11, we began the array daytab with a column of zero. This is more obvious than changing the indices because space is not an issue here.

The number of rows is unimportant since what is supplied is, as before, a pointer to an array of rows, where each row is an array of 13 ints. If a two-dimensional array is to be passed to a function, the parameter declaration in the function must include the number of columns; the number of rows is immaterial. It is a pointer to objects in this example that are arrays of 13 ints. So, if the function f is to be called with the array daytab as a parameter, the declaration of f would be: f(intdaytab[2][13]) ...

Since the number of rows is unimportant, it might also be f(intdaytab[][13]) or f(int (*daytab)[13]), which indicates that the parameter is a reference to an array of 13 numbers. Because brackets [] have priority over *, the brackets are required. The declaration int *daytab[13] is an array of 13 pointers to integers without any parenthesis. In general, an array only has one free dimension (the subscript); all the others must be provided.

Initialization of Pointer Arrays

A month_name(n) function that returns a pointer to a character string holding the name of the n-th month is a challenge to write. An internal static array works best in this situation. When called, month_name provides a pointer to the appropriate character string from a private array of character strings it contains. This section demonstrates the initialization of an array of names. Similar to earlier initializations, the syntax is as follows:

```
char *month_name(int n)

{

static char *name[] = {

"Illegal month",

"January", "February", "March",

"April", "May", "June",

"July", "August", "September",

"October", "November", "December"

};

return (n < 1 || n > 12) ? name[0] : name[n];

}
```

Name, an array of character pointers, has the same declaration as lineptri in the sorting example. Each character string in the initializer is given the appropriate location in the array. A pointer to the characters of the i-th string are located somewhere and are saved in name[i]. The compiler counts the initializers and enters the proper amount because the size of the array name is not given.

Pointers vs. Multi-dimensional Arrays

The distinction between a two-dimensional array and an array of pointers, such as name in the example above, might occasionally baffle C beginners. The definitions suggest

```
int a[10][20];

int *b[10];
```

then references to a single int are both syntactically valid in positions a[3][4] and b[3][4]. A real two-dimensional array, however, is a: The element a[row,col] is found using the traditional rectangular subscript calculation 20 * row + col, which has been reserved for 200 int-sized locations. The definition only creates 10 pointers for b, however, and does not initialise any of them; initialization must be done explicitly, either statically or through code. There will be 200 ints set aside, plus ten cells for the pointers, assuming that each element of b does point to a twenty-element array. The fact that the rows of the array can be different lengths is a key benefit of the pointer array. That is, not every element of b must point to a vector of twenty elements; some elements may point to two, some to fifty, and some to none. Although we have framed this topic in terms of numbers, the storage of character strings of various lengths, as in the function month_name, is by far the most common application of arrays of pointers. For an array of pointers, compare the declaration and the illustration:

char *name[] = { "Illegal month", "Jan", "Feb", "Mar" };

with those for a two-dimensional array:

char aname[][15] = { "Illegal month", "Jan", "Feb", "Mar" };

Array of Pointers

Pointers can be used as the elements of an array that we can declare. array of pointer declaration syntax: datatype *arrayname[size];

For instance, we can write int *a[10] to declare an array of size 20 that contains integer pointers, and we can initialise each element of a[] with variable addresses.

Functions returning Pointer

A function that produces a pointer can exist. To declare this type of function, use the syntax type *function_name(type1,type2,......); For Example: void main()
{
int *p;
p=fun();

}
int *fun() {
int a=5;
int *q=&a;
------------------------- return q;

}

Pointers to Functions

How to declare a pointer to a function?

sentence structure: returntype_of_function (*pointer variable)(list of arguments); For instance, the expression int (*p)(int,int); can be understood to mean that p is a pointer to a function that accepts two integer arguments and has an integer return type.

How to make a pointer to a function?

Syntax:

pointer_variable=function_name_without_parantheses; For Example:

p=test;

can be read as p is a pointer to function test.

How to call a function using pointer?

Syntax:

pointer_variable(ist of arguments);

OR

(*pointer_variable)(List of arguments);

The following program illustrates pointer to function

```c
int getc()
{
return 10; }
void put(int a)
{
printf("%d",a);
}
void main()
{
int k;
int (*p)(); /*You can write void *p();*/ void (*q)(int); /*You can write void *q(int);*/ p=get;
q=put; k=p(); q(k);
}
```

NOTE:

(i) In the C programming language, each function's entry point is encoded in the function name along with its physical memory location. The base address of the function is copied into the pointer if you assign it a pointer. By using this control, you can switch between calling and being called by functions.

(ii) All functions are accessible from wherever by default because they are global. Therefore, there is no reason to build a pointer function.

A function is not a variable in C, but pointers to functions can be defined and assigned, put in arrays, supplied to functions, returned by functions, and other things. To demonstrate this, we will change the sorting method described earlier in this chapter so that it will sort the input lines numerically rather than lexicographically in the event that the optional argument -n is provided.

The three components of a sort are frequently a comparison to determine the ordering of each pair of objects, an exchange to reverse the order of the objects, and a sorting algorithm to continue comparing and exchanging the objects until they are in the correct order. We can sort by various criteria by providing various comparison and exchange functions to the sorting algorithm, which is independent of comparison and exchange processes. This strategy is used in our new sort. Strcmp, like before, compares two lines lexicographically; moreover, we'll need a routine called numcmp that compares two lines based on numerical value and provides the same kind of condition indicator as strcmp. These functions are defined before main, and qsort receives a pointer to the appropriate one. In order to focus on the important concerns, we have cut back on the processing of arguments' errors.

```c
#include <stdio.h>
#include <string.h>
#define MAXLINES 5000 /* max #lines to be sorted */
char *lineptr[MAXLINES]; /* pointers to text lines */
int readlines(char *lineptr[], intnlines);
void writelines(char *lineptr[], intnlines);
void qsort(void *lineptr[], int left, int right, int (*comp)(void *, void *));
int numcmp(char *, char *);
/* sort input lines */
```

```c
main(intargc, char *argv[])
{
intnlines; /* number of input lines read */ int numeric = 0; /* 1 if numeric sort */
if (argc> 1 &&strcmp(argv[1], "-n") == 0) numeric = 1;
if ((nlines = readlines(lineptr, MAXLINES)) >= 0)
{
qsort((void**) lineptr, 0, nlines-1,
(int (*)(void*,void*))(numeric ? numcmp : strcmp)); writelines(lineptr, nlines);
return 0;
}
else
{
printf("input too big to sort\n");
return 1;
}
}
```

Strcmp and numcmp compare function addresses while calling qsort. The & is not required because it is understood that they are functions, just as it is not required before an array name. We created qsorts to handle all types of data, not simply character strings. Qsort anticipates an array of pointers, two integers, and a function with two pointer arguments, as shown by the function prototype. The pointer arguments are of the generic pointer type void *. We can call qsortby converting arguments to void * because any pointer may be cast to void * and back again without losing any information. The comparison function's arguments are cast using the function argument's intricate cast. These will typically not affect the actual representation but will reassure the compiler that everything is in order.

```c
void qsort(void *v[], int left, int right,
int (*comp)(void *, void *))
{
inti, last;
void swap(void *v[], int, int);
```

```
if (left >= right) /* do nothing if array contains */ return; /* fewer than two elements */
swap(v, left, (left + right)/2);
last = left;
for (i = left+1; i<= right; i++) if ((*comp)(v[i], v[left]) < 0) swap(v, ++last, i);
swap(v, left, last);
qsort(v, left, last-1, comp); qsort(v, last+1, right, comp);
}
```

The declarations should be carefully read. Int (*comp)(void *, void *) is the fourth parameter of the qsort function, indicating that comp is a reference to a function with two void * arguments and an int return value.

The declaration is consistent with the use of comp in the line if ((*comp)(v[i], v[left]) 0): comp is a reference to a function, *comp is the function, and (*comp)(v[i], v[left]) is the call to it. Without the brackets, int *comp(void *, void *) claims that comp is a function returning a reference to an int, which is a quite different statement from what it actually means. Strcmp, which compares two strings, has already been demonstrated. Here is numcmp, which was generated by calling atof and compares two strings on a leading numeric value:

```
#include <stdlib.h>
/* numcmp: compare s1 and s2 numerically */
intnumcmp(char *s1, char *s2)
{ double v1, v2; v1 = atof(s1);
v2 = atof(s2);
if (v1 < v2) return -1;
else if (v1 > v2) return 1;
else
return 0;
}
```

The swap function, which exchanges two pointers, is as follows

```
void swap(void *v[], inti, int j;)
{ void *temp; temp = v[i]; v[i] = v[j]; v[j] = temp;
}
```

assigns a character array pointer to pmessage. There are only pointers involved; this is not a string copy. There are no operators in C that can handle a whole string of characters at once. Between these definitions, there is a significant distinction:

char amessage[] = "now is the time";

char *pmessage = "now is the time";

Amessage is an array that is only large enough to accommodate the character string and '0' used to initialise it. Although the array's individual letters are changeable, a message will always refer to the same storage. Pmessage, on the other hand, is a pointer that is initialised to refer to a constant string. You can change the pointer's location later, but if you try to change the text's contents, the outcome is undefined.

By examining modified versions of two practical functions taken from the standard library, we will show additional features of pointers and arrays. Strcpy(s,t) is the first function, and it copies the string t to the string s. While saying s=t would be good, doing so copies the pointer rather than the characters. We require a loop in order to replicate the characters. First, the array version:

void strcpy(char *s, char *t)

{

inti;

i = 0;

while ((s[i] = t[i]) != '\0') i++;

}

For contrast, here is a version of strcpywith pointers:

void strcpy(char *s, char *t)

{

inti; i = 0;

while ((*s = *t) != '\0')

{ s++; t++; }

}

The parameters s and t can be used whenever strcpy sees fit because arguments are supplied by value. Here, they are provided with neatly initialised pointers that are marched down the arrays one character at a time until the '0' that ends t has been copied into s. Strcpy would not be written as we demonstrated above in real life. The preferred syntax for experienced C programmers is void strcpy(char *s, char *t).

```c
{
while ((*s++ = *t++) != '\0')
;
}
```

As a result, the increment of s and t is moved into the loop's test section. The character that t originally pointed to before it was increased is the value of *t++; the postfix ++ doesn't modify t until this character has been fetched. The character is also stored into the former s place before s is increased in the same manner. In order to regulate the loop, this character's value is also compared to "0." Overall, characters up to and including the last "0" are copied from t to s.

The comparison against "0" in the final abbreviation is unnecessary because the only thing being asked is whether the expression is zero. The function would therefore probably be written as void strcpy(char *s, char *t)

```c
{
while (*s++ = *t++)
;
}
```

Although this may initially appear confusing, the notational convenience is significant, and the phrase should be grasped since you will regularly encounter it in C programmes. The standard library's (string.h) strcpy function returns the target string as the value of its function. The second procedure we'll look at is strcmp(s,t), which compares the character strings s and t and returns true or false depending on whether s is lexicographically bigger or less than t. The value is calculated by removing the characters where s and t don't agree in the first place.

```c
int strcmp(char *s, char *t)
{
inti;
for (i = 0; s[i] == t[i]; i++) if (s[i] == '\0')
return 0;
return s[i] - t[i];
```

}

The pointer version of strcmp:

int strcmp(char *s, char *t)

{

for (; *s == *t; s++, t++) if (*s == '\0')

return 0;

return *s - *t;

}

There are other, less common pairings of * and ++ and -- because ++ and -- are either prefix or postfix operators. For instance, before obtaining the character that p points to, *--p decreases p. The typical idiom for pushing and popping a stack is really the pair of expressions *p++ = val; val = *--p; The header string.h> provides declarations for the functions covered in this section as well as a number of other string-handling functions from the standard library.

Pointer Arrays; Pointers to Pointers

Datatype (*pointer_variable)[size] is the syntax to specify a pointer to an array; For instance, int (*ptr)[10];Here, ptr is a pointer that can point to an array of 10 integers. We can initialise ptr with the array's base address and then access different elements of the array by increasing ptr's value.

Pointers can be stored in arrays exactly like other variables because they are variables in and of themselves. As an example, let's create a streamlined version of the UNIX programme sort that would alphabetically arrange a set of text lines.

We require a data format that can easily and effectively handle text lines of different lengths. The array of pointers enters at this point. Each line can be accessed by a pointer to its initial character if the lines to be sorted are stored end to end in one lengthy character array. The actual pointers can be kept in an array. By providing the pointers of two lines to strcmp, two lines can be compared. The pointers in the pointer array are switched out instead of the actual text lines when two out-of-order lines need to be exchanged.

By doing this, the twin issues of difficult storage management and significant overhead associated with moving the lines themselves are avoided.

Three steps make up the sorting procedure:

read all the lines of input

sort them

print them in order

The programme should, as usual, be divided into functions that correspond to this natural division, with the main routine managing the other functions. Deferring the sorting process will allow us to focus on the data structure, input, and output for the time being. Each line's characters must be collected, saved, and an array of pointers to the lines must be created by the input routine. It will also need to count the number of input lines because sorting and printing depend on that data. Since the input function can only handle a limited number of input lines, it may return an illegal value, such as -1, if there is an excessive amount of input. Only the lines in the array of pointers' order must be printed by the output procedure.

```c
#include <stdio.h>
#include <string.h>
#define MAXLINES 5000
char *lineptr[MAXLINES];
intreadlines(char *lineptr[], intnlines);
void writelines(char *lineptr[], intnlines);
void qsort(char *lineptr[], int left, int right); main()
{
intnlines;
if ((nlines = readlines(lineptr, MAXLINES)) >= 0) { qsort(lineptr, 0, nlines-1);
writelines(lineptr, nlines); return 0;
} else {
printf("error: input too big to sort\n");
return 1;
}
}
#define MAXLEN 1000
intgetline(char *, int);
char *alloc(int);
intreadlines(char *lineptr[], intmaxlines)
```

```c
{
intlen, nlines;
char *p, line[MAXLEN];
nlines = 0;
while ((len = getline(line, MAXLEN)) > 0)
if (nlines>= maxlines || p = alloc(len) == NULL) return -1;
else {
line[len-1] = '\0'; /* delete newline */ strcpy(p, line);
lineptr[nlines++] = p;
}
return nlines;
}
void writelines(char *lineptr[], intnlines)
{
inti;
for (i = 0; i<nlines; i++) printf("%s\n", lineptr[i]);
}
```

The declaration for lineptr, which reads char *lineptr[MAXLINES], is the key innovation. It specifies that lineptr is an array of MAXLINES items, each of which is a pointer to a char. In other words, *lineptr[i] is the character it points to, the first character of the i-th stored text line, and lineptr[i] is a character pointer.

Lineptri can be considered as a pointer in the same way as in our earlier instances as it is the name of an array itself, and writelines can be written as

```c
void writelines(char *lineptr[], intnlines)
{
while (nlines-- > 0) printf("%s\n", *lineptr++);
}
```

*lineptr initially points to the first line; when nlines is counted down, each element moves it to the next line pointer.

We can go on to sorting after input and output are under control.

(char *v[, int left, int right) void

{

inti, last;

void swap(char *v[], inti, int j);

if (left >= right) /* do nothing if array contains */ return; /* fewer than two elements */

swap(v, left, (left + right)/2);

last = left;

for (i = left+1; i<= right; i++) if (strcmp(v[i], v[left]) < 0) swap(v, ++last, i);

swap(v, left, last);

qsort(v, left, last-1);

qsort(v, last+1, right);

}

Similarly, the swap routine needs only trivial changes:

void swap(char *v[], inti, int j)

{

char *temp; temp = v[i];

v[i] = v[j]; v[j] = temp;

}

Since temp must be a character pointer in order for one to be transferred to the other, every element of v (also known as lineptr) must be one as well.

Multi-dimensional Arrays

Although C offers rectangular multi-dimensional arrays, pointer arrays are utilised much more frequently in practise. We shall demonstrate some of their characteristics in this section.

Take into account the issue of converting dates from a day of the month to a day of the year and vice versa. For instance, March 1 falls on a non-leap year's 60th day and a leap year's 61st day.

Let's construct two functions to perform the conversions: month_day translates the day of the year into the month and day, and day_of_year turns the month and day into the day of the year. Because of the computation of two values by the later function, the month and day parameters will be pointers:

month_day(1988, 60, &m, &d)

sets m to 2 and d to 29 (February 29th).

Both of these services require the same data, a table with the number of days in each month (e.g., "September has thirty days," etc.). It is simpler to divide the months into two rows of a two-dimensional array than to keep track of what happens to February throughout calculation because the number of days in each month varies for leap years and non-leap years. The functions and array used for the transformations are as follows:

```c
static char daytab[2][13] = {
{0, 31, 28, 31, 30, 31, 30, 31, 31, 30, 31, 30, 31},
{0, 31, 29, 31, 30, 31, 30, 31, 31, 30, 31, 30, 31}
};
intday_of_year(int year, int month, int day)
{
inti, leap;
leap = year%4 == 0 && year%100 != 0 || year%400 == 0; for (i = 1; i< month; i++)
day += daytab[leap][i];
return day;
}
void month_day(int year, intyearday, int *pmonth, int *pday)
{
inti, leap;
leap = year%4 == 0 && year%100 != 0 || year%400 == 0; for (i = 1; yearday>daytab[leap][i]; i++)
yearday -= daytab[leap][i];
*pmonth = i;
*pday = yearday;
}
```

Remember that a logical expression, like the one for leap, can be used as a subscript of the array daytab since its arithmetic value is either zero (false) or one (true).

Both day_of_year and month_day can use the array daytab because it is external to both of those variables. We changed it to char to show how small non-character integers can be stored using char. The first two-dimensional array we dealt with was daytab. A two-dimensional array in C is actually a one-dimensional array with arrays as its elements. As a result, subscripts are written as daytab[i][j] instead of daytab[i,j].

A two-dimensional array can be processed in much the same way as in other languages, save from this notational difference. The rightmost subscript or column varies the quickest as elements are retrieved in storage order since elements are stored by rows.

A list of initializers enclosed in braces is used to initialise an array, and a corresponding sub-list is used to initialise each row of a two-dimensional array. Since month numbers naturally range from 1 to 12 rather than 0 to 11, we began the array daytab with a column of zero. This is more obvious than changing the indices because space is not an issue here.

The number of rows is unimportant since what is supplied is, as before, a pointer to an array of rows, where each row is an array of 13 ints. If a two-dimensional array is to be passed to a function, the parameter declaration in the function must include the number of columns; the number of rows is immaterial. It is a pointer to objects in this example that are arrays of 13 ints. As a result, the declaration of f would be as follows if the array daytabis to be supplied to f: f(intdaytab[2][13]) { ... }

Since the number of rows is unimportant, it might also be f(intdaytab[][13]) or f(int (*daytab)[13]), which indicates that the parameter is a reference to an array of 13 numbers. Because brackets [] have priority over *, the brackets are required. The declaration int *daytab[13] is an array of 13 pointers to integers without any parenthesis. In general, an array only has one free dimension (the subscript); all the others must be provided.

Initialization of Pointer Arrays

A month_name(n) function that returns a pointer to a character string holding the name of the n-th month is a challenge to write. An internal static array works best in this situation. When called, month_name provides a pointer to the appropriate character string from a private array of character strings it contains. This section demonstrates the initialization of an array of names. Similar to earlier initializations, the syntax is as follows:

char *month_name(int n)

{

static char *name[] = {

"Illegal month",

"January", "February", "March",

"April", "May", "June",

"July", "August", "September",

"October", "November", "December"

};

return (n < 1 || n > 12) ? name[0] : name[n];

}

Name, an array of character pointers, has the same declaration as lineptri in the sorting example. Each character string in the initializer is given the appropriate location in the array. A pointer to the characters of the i-th string are located somewhere and are saved in name[i]. The compiler counts the initializers and enters the proper amount because the size of the array name is not given.

Pointers vs. Multi-dimensional Arrays

The distinction between a two-dimensional array and an array of pointers, such as name in the example above, might occasionally baffle C beginners. Assuming that int a[10][20] and int *b[10] have the same meanings, then a[3][4] and b[3][4] are both syntactically legitimate references to a single int. A real two-dimensional array, however, is a: The element a[row,col] is found using the traditional rectangular subscript calculation 20 * row + col, which has been reserved for 200 int-sized locations. The definition only creates 10 pointers for b, however, and does not initialise any of them; initialization must be done explicitly, either statically or through code. There will be 200 ints set aside, plus ten cells for the pointers, assuming that each element of b does point to a twenty-element array. The fact that the rows of the array can be different lengths is a key benefit of the pointer array. That is, not every element of b must point to a vector of twenty elements; some elements may point to two, some to fifty, and some to none. Although we have framed this topic in terms of numbers, the storage of character strings of various lengths, as in the function month_name, is by far the most common application of arrays of pointers. For an array of pointers, compare the declaration and the illustration:

char *name[] = { "Illegal month", "Jan", "Feb", "Mar" };

with those for a two-dimensional array:

char aname[][15] = { "Illegal month", "Jan", "Feb", "Mar" };

Array of Pointers

Pointers can be used as the elements of an array that we can declare. array of pointer declaration syntax: datatype *arrayname[size];

For instance, we can write int *a[10] to declare an array of size 20 that contains integer pointers, and we can initialise each element of a[] with variable addresses.

Functions returning Pointer

A function that produces a pointer can exist. To declare this type of function, use the syntax type *function_name(type1,type2,......); For Example: void main()

{

int *p;

p=fun();

}

int *fun() {

int a=5;

int *q=&a;

-------------------------- return q;

}

Pointers to Functions

How to declare a pointer to a function?

Syntax: returntype_of_function (*pointer variable)(List of arguments); For example:

int (*p)(int,int); can be interpreted as p is a pointer to function which takes two integers as argument and returntype is integer.

How to make a pointer to a function?

Syntax:

pointer_variable=function_name_without_parantheses; For Example:

p=test;

can be read as p is a pointer to function test.

How to call a function using pointer?

Syntax:

pointer_variable(ist of arguments);

OR

(*pointer_variable)(List of arguments);

The following program illustrates pointer to function

```
int getc()
{
return 10; }
void put(int a)
{
printf("%d",a);
}
void main()
{
int k;
int (*p)(); /*You can write void *p();*/ void (*q)(int); /*You can write void *q(int);*/ p=get;
q=put; k=p(); q(k);
}
```

NOTE:

(i) In the C programming language, each function's entry point is encoded in the function name along with its physical memory location. The base address of the function is copied into the pointer if you assign it a pointer. By using this control, you can switch between calling and being called by functions.

(ii) All functions are accessible from wherever by default because they are global. Therefore, there is no reason to build a pointer function.

A function is not a variable in C, but pointers to functions can be defined and assigned, put in arrays, supplied to functions, returned by functions, and other things. To demonstrate this, we will change the sorting method described earlier in this chapter so that it will sort the input lines numerically rather than lexicographically in the event that the optional argument -n is provided.

The three components of a sort are frequently a comparison to determine the ordering of each pair of objects, an exchange to reverse the order of the objects, and a sorting algorithm to continue comparing and exchanging the objects until they are in the correct order. We can sort by various criteria by providing various comparison and exchange functions to the sorting algorithm, which is independent of comparison and exchange processes. This strategy is used in our new sort. Strcmp, like previously, compares two lines lexicographically; moreover, we'll need numcmp, which compares two lines based on numerical value and provides the same kind of condition indicator as strcmpdoes. These functions are defined before main, and qsort receives a pointer to the appropriate one. In order to focus on the important concerns, we have cut back on the processing of arguments' errors.

```c
#include <stdio.h>
#include <string.h>
#define MAXLINES 5000 /* max #lines to be sorted */
char *lineptr[MAXLINES]; /* pointers to text lines */
int readlines(char *lineptr[], intnlines);
void writelines(char *lineptr[], intnlines);
void qsort(void *lineptr[], int left, int right, int (*comp)(void *, void *));
int numcmp(char *, char *);
/* sort input lines */
main(intargc, char *argv[])
{
intnlines; /* number of input lines read */ int numeric = 0; /* 1 if numeric sort */
if (argc> 1 &&strcmp(argv[1], "-n") == 0) numeric = 1;
if ((nlines = readlines(lineptr, MAXLINES)) >= 0)
{
qsort((void**) lineptr, 0, nlines-1,
(int (*)(void*,void*))(numeric ? numcmp : strcmp)); writelines(lineptr, nlines);
return 0;
}
else
```

```
{
printf("input too big to sort\n");
return 1;
}
}
```

Strcmp and numcmp compare function addresses while calling qsort. The & is not required because it is understood that they are functions, just as it is not required before an array name. We created qsorts to handle all types of data, not simply character strings. Qsort anticipates an array of pointers, two integers, and a function with two pointer arguments, as shown by the function prototype. The pointer arguments are of the generic pointer type void *. We can call qsortby converting arguments to void * because any pointer may be cast to void * and back again without losing any information. The comparison function's arguments are cast using the function argument's intricate cast. These will typically not affect the actual representation but will reassure the compiler that everything is in order.

```
void qsort(void *v[], int left, int right,
int (*comp)(void *, void *))
{
inti, last;
void swap(void *v[], int, int);
if (left >= right) /* do nothing if array contains */ return; /* fewer than two elements */
swap(v, left, (left + right)/2);
last = left;
for (i = left+1; i<= right; i++) if ((*comp)(v[i], v[left]) < 0) swap(v, ++last, i);
swap(v, left, last);
qsort(v, left, last-1, comp); qsort(v, last+1, right, comp);
}
```

The declarations should be carefully read. Int (*comp)(void *, void *) is the fourth parameter of the qsort function, indicating that comp is a reference to a function with two void * arguments and an int return value.

The declaration is consistent with the use of comp in the line if ((*comp)(v[i], v[left]) 0): comp is a reference to a function, *comp is the function, and (*comp)(v[i], v[left]) is the call to it. Without the brackets, int *comp(void *, void *) claims that comp is a function returning a reference to an int, which is a quite different statement from what it actually means. Strcmp, which compares two strings, has already been demonstrated. Here is numcmp, which was generated by calling atof and compares two strings on a leading numeric value:

```c
#include <stdlib.h>
/* numcmp: compare s1 and s2 numerically */
intnumcmp(char *s1, char *s2)
{ double v1, v2; v1 = atof(s1);
v2 = atof(s2);
if (v1 < v2) return -1;
else if (v1 > v2) return 1;
else
return 0;
}
```

The swap function, which exchanges two pointers, is as follows

```c
void swap(void *v[], inti, int j;)
{ void *temp; temp = v[i]; v[i] = v[j]; v[j] = temp;
}
```

Chapter 31: DYNAMIC MEMORY ALLOCATION

Static memory allocation was used up until this point in the process. The programme could now use the fixed amount of RAM. As a result, we were unable to allocate or free up memory while the programme was running. It is impossible to foresee how much memory the programme will require when it is running. For illustration, let's say we've declared a fixed-size array with 20 members. As a result, memory is wasted if the number of values to be stored in an array at runtime is less than 20, and our programme may crash if the array has more than 20 values. We use dynamic memory allocation to address the aforementioned issues and allot RAM while running.

The following functions are used in dynamic memory allocation and are defined in <stdlib.h>

1. malloc()

Declaration: void *malloc(size_t size);

For dynamic memory allocation, use this function. The amount of bytes to be allocated is specified by the argument size. A pointer to the first byte of allocated memory is returned by malloc() on success. The pointer that was returned is of type void, but it can be type cast to another type of pointer if necessary. Malloc() allocated memory contains junk values.

2. calloc()

Declaration: void *calloc(size_t n,size_t size);

Memory can be allocated in several blocks using this function. Both the first and second arguments specify the number of blocks and the size of each block, respectively. Calloc() initialises the memory it allots to zero.

3. realloc()

Declaration: void *realloc(void *ptr,size_t newsize);

The size of the memory block can be changed using the realloc() method. The memory block's size is changed without erasing any previous data. The first argument to this function is a pointer to the memory block that was previously allocated by calling mallloc() or calloc(), and the second argument is the block's new size.

4. free();

Declaration: void free(void *p);

The dynamically allocated memory space is released using this function. The heap is given access to the memory that was released by free() once more so that it can be used for other purposes. Any memory space that has not been allocated by malloc(), calloc(), or realloc() should not be attempted to be freed.

The allocation of dynamic memory is demonstrated in the programme below.

```c
#include<stdio.h> #include<stdlib.h> void main()
{
int *p,n,i;
printf("Enter the number of integers to be entered"); scanf("%d",&n);
p=(int *)malloc(n*sizeof(int)); /* This is same as "(int *)calloc(n,sizeof(int))"*/
/* If we write "(int *)malloc(sizeof(int))" then only 2 byte of memory will be allocated dynamically*/
if(p==NULL)
{
printf("Memory is not available"); exit(1);
}
for(i=0;i<n;i++)
{
printf("Enter an integer"); scanf("%d",p+i);
}
for(i=0;i<n;i++) printf("%d\t",*(p+i));
}
```

Chapter 32: POINTER TO STRUCTURES

You might remember that an array's name corresponds to the address of its zeroth element. The same is valid for structure variable array names.

Consider the declaration:

struct stud {

int roll;

char dept_code[25]; float cgpa;

} class[100], *ptr ;

The address of the structure array's zeroth element is represented by the name class. A pointer to data items of the type struct stud is represented by ptr. The address of class[0] will be assigned to ptr by the assignment ptr = class.

After one is added to the pointer (ptr++):

Sizeof(stud) actually raises the value of ptr.

It's designed to point to the following record.

The members can be accessed as follows once ptr points to a structural variable:

ptr –> roll;

ptr –> dept_code; ptr –> cgpa;

The symbol "–>" is called the arrow operator.

A file is a group of data kept on a secondary storage medium, such as a hard drive. All of the input data is combined during a file action, which the C programme then uses to perform its operations. A file can be subjected to numerous operations, including insertion, deletion, opening and closing. In C programming, all data is lost when the programme is closed. It takes a lot of time to enter all of the data if you want to keep a lot of it. However, these details can be obtained with a few instructions if a file is generated. In the C language, there are numerous functions that deal with file I/O. You will learn how to manage standard I/O (High level file I/O functions) in C in this course. High level file operations fall into the following categories:

1. Text file

2. Binary file

There are various ways to open a file for these activities. The different modes include open a text file so you may read it.

w truncate to zero length or create a text file for writing

a append; open or create text file for writing at end-of-file

rb open binary file for reading

wb truncate to zero length or create a binary file for writing

ab append; open or create binary file for writing at end-of-file

r+ open text file for update (reading and writing)

w+ truncate to zero length or create a text file for update

a+ append; open or create text file for update

r+b or rb+ open binary file for update (reading and writing)

w+b or wb+ truncate to zero length or create a binary file for update

a+b or ab+ append; open or create binary file for update

Fopen and freopen associate a stream with the file whose name is in the string pointed to by filename. Both operations return a pointer to the object managing the stream or a null pointer if the open action fails. If the open operation fails, the error and end-of-file (EOF) indications are reset. In contrast to fopen, freopen ignores any close errors and closes any open files first while they are already open.

Q1. Write a program to open a file using fopen().

Ans:

```c
#include<stdio.h> void main()
{
fopen() file *fp;
fp=fopen("student.DAT", "r");
if(fp==NULL)
{
printf("The file could not be open"); exit(0);
}
```

Q2. Write a C program to read name and marks of n number of students from user and store them in a file. If the file previously exits, add the information of n students.

Ans:

```c
#include <stdio.h>
int main()
{
char name[50]; int marks, i,n;
printf("Enter number of students");
scanf("%d", &n);
FILE *fptr;
fptr=(fopen("C:\\student.txt","a"));
if (fptr==NULL){ printf("Error!"); exit(1);
}
for(i=0;i<n;++i)
{ printf("For student%d\nEnter name: ",i+1); scanf("%s",name);
printf("Enter marks");
scanf("%d", &marks);
```

fprintf(fptr, "\nName: %s\nMarks=%d\n", name, marks);

} fclose(fptr);

Return 0;

}

The corresponding file is closed as well as the stream pointed to by the fclose function. Any buffered data for the stream that has not yet been written to is sent to the host environment to be written to the file; any buffered data that has not yet been read is discarded. The stream and file are no longer connected. The corresponding buffer is deallocated if it was automatically allocated. If the stream was closed properly, the method returns zero; otherwise, it returns EOF.

Q.3. Write a program to read data from file and close using fclose function.

Ans:

#include <stdio.h> int main()

int n

FILE *fptr;

if ((fptr=fopen("C:\\program.txt","r"))==NULL){ printf("Error! opening file");

exit(1); // Program exits if file pointer returns NULL.

}

fscanf(fptr,"%d",&n); printf("Value of n=%d",n); fclose(fptr);

return 0;

}

Q4. Write a C program to write all the members of an array of strcures to a file using fwrite(). Read the array from the file and display on the screen.

Ans:

#include<stdio.h>

Struct s

{

Char name[50];

Int height;

};

Int main()

```c
{
Struct s a[5], b[5];
FILE *fptr;
Int I;
Fptr=fopen("file.txt", "wb");
For(i=0; i<5; ++i)
{
fflush(stdin);
printf("Enter name: ") ; gets(a[i].name); printf("Enter height: "); scanf("%d",&a[i].height);
}
fwrite(a,sizeof(a),1,fptr);    fclose(fptr);    fptr=fopen("file.txt","rb");    fread(b,sizeof(b),1,fptr);
for(i=0;i<5;++i)
{
printf("Name: %s\nHeight: %d",b[i].name,b[i].height);
} fclose(fptr);
}
```

Chapter 34: ALGORITHM AND DATA STRUCTURE

Algorithm

- An algorithm is a method for addressing a problem step-by-step.
- It is defined as any clearly defined computing process that accepts an input value and outputs an output value within a finite time frame.
- Several algorithms can be developed to address a same issue.

Real world applications of algorithms

☐ The Human Genome project

☐ The Internet

☐ E-commerce

Data Structure

- A data structure is a means to arrange data so that it is easier to access and modify.
- For instance, a structure stores data of many types, whereas an array progressively stores data of similar types. These two are the foundational data structures that additional data structures are built upon.
- As an illustration, we could design a structure to house student information. The information for numerous pupils will be stored in an array of such a structure. Thus, another data structure will be represented by this array of structures.
- Stack, queue, linked list, trees, and other well-known data structures are also available.
- Understanding diverse data structures is crucial since no one data structure is suitable for all uses.

Difference between algorithm and data structure

- A data structure is a way to store similar or heterogeneous data, whereas an algorithm is a way to solve a problem.
- Each algorithm must operate on a particular data structure, such as an array, tree, or list.

- In plainer terms, a data structure is a method of storing data, and an algorithm is a method of accessing and modifying that data.

Properties of Algorithm

The following attributes must be present in an algorithm.

- Input: An algorithm must accept at least one (maybe more) value as an input.
- Output: An algorithm needs to create some specific results.
- Finiteness: An algorithm must come to a conclusion after a set amount of steps.
- Definiteness: An algorithm should be definite, meaning that there should be no ambiguity at any point in the process.
- Effectiveness: It must be possible to follow an algorithm's steps without using any intelligence.

Types of algorithm

Typically, algorithms can be divided into two groups:

- Iterative: These algorithms use loops and conditional expressions to sequentially execute the input.

  Example: Linear search
- Recursive: These algorithms address smaller problems by breaking up a larger problem into smaller ones. They then integrate the outcomes of the lesser challenges to address the primary issue at hand.

Chapter 35: ANALYSIS OF ALGORITHMS

As was previously said, numerous algorithms can be developed to address a particular issue. The best algorithm is always preferred. Efficiency can be measured in terms of the amount of time or space needed to solve an issue.

Algorithm analysis is a method for comparing the relative efficacy of several algorithms. The time needed to solve a problem cannot be represented clearly in terms of the number of seconds needed because the speed of an algorithm can vary between computers (depending on computer performance). Instead, the amount of calculations needed to solve the issue is what is quantified.

The actual number of operations is not used in real-world circumstances. Instead, a mathematical function of the input size is used to represent how long something will take. The growth rate of that function is used to compare two algorithms. The algorithm will take longer as the input size grows if the growth rate is higher.

Representation of analysis

Big-O notation is typically used to denote the mathematical function. An asymptotic upper bound of the function is provided by Big-O notation.

Consider making the function a polynomial function.

$F(n) = a, b,..., z$, where n is the variable and a, b,..., z are the coefficients.

The function is expanding rapidly. It surpasses all polynomial equations with powers lower than k. However, it is less than any polynomial with a power higher than k.

Therefore, $F(n)$ $n(k+1)$ and so forth.

Additionally, we can always locate a constant such that $F(n) = nk$.

Therefore, the values nk, n(k+1), and so forth reflect an upper bound on the function. It is symbolically denoted as $F(n)= O (nk)$, $F(n)= O (nk+1)$, and so on.

Definition of Big-O

If a positive constant c exists for the two functions $F(n)$ and $G(n)$, then

$0 <= F(n) <= c\ G(n)$, for some $n>=n0$

Then $F(n)=O(G(n))$

Other representations

- Big-Ω :

This provides a function's asymptotic lower bound.

Informally, it is the shortest amount of time an algorithm will require to complete a task.

If a positive constant c exists for the two functions F(n) and G(n), then

- $\leq c\ G(n) \leq F(n)$, for some n>=n0

Then F(n)= Ω (G(n))

- Big-Θ:

For two functions F(n) and G(n), if there exists two positive constant c1 and c2, such that

- $0 \leq c1\ G(n) \leq F(n) \leq c2\ G(n)$, for some n>=n0

Then F(n)= Θ (G(n))

Comparison of speed of two algorithms (an example)

A and B are two hypothetical computers. If A can process 10 instructions per second and B can process 10 instructions per second, respectively. Two algorithms, one with a time complexity of 2n2 and the other 50nlogn, should exist to solve a given issue. Let the quicker computer A run the first algorithm and the slower computer B the second algorithm.

When input size n=10^7,

Time required by computer A = 2 x (10^7)^2 / 10^10

= 20000 seconds (about 5.5 hours)

Time required by computer B = 50 x (10^7) x log(10^7) / 10^10

= 1163 seconds (less than 20 minutes)

Even though the first computer was around 1000 times faster than the second, it took much longer to complete an algorithm with a higher level of complexity.

Cases considered in analysis

- Best case : This analysis is performed when the input is favourable to the outcome.

  For instance, in a sorting problem, best case analysis refers to the analysis performed after the list has already been sorted.

  There is not much interest in this.

- Worst case: Worst case analysis measures how long an algorithm takes to run for a specific size of input.

  The worst case scenario for a sorting issue is when the numbers have previously been sorted, but in reverse order.

This provides an algorithm's upper bound.

- □ Average case :

    It is the general case (not best not worst).

    But in practice, it is as bad as the worst case.

    It occurs fairly often (as often as worst case).

In sorting example, sorting any random list falls under this category.

An example of finding time complexity

Consider the following code snippet for sorting an array.

```
for(i=0;i<n;i++)
for(j=i+1;j<n;j++)
if(arr[i]>arr[j])
swap(arr[i],arr[j]);
```

The first element is contrasted with the remaining n-1 items in this case, the second element with the remaining n-2 elements, and so on.

As a result, the total number of comparisons is (n-1) + (n-2) +... + 1 = n(n-1)/2.

This polynomial equation has a power of two. The algorithm is thus described as being O(n2).

Chapter 36: STORAGE STRUCTURE OF ARRAYS

Storage structure of arrays:

- Linear data structures called arrays are used to hold homogeneous elements in clusters of memory.
- Every location in memory has an address. In essence, the address is an integer.
- Each member of the array will be stored at x locations separate from its predecessor and successor if more than one memory address is needed to store a value of a certain data type (let's say x number of locations).
- Consider a group of five characters, each of which requires one byte of storage (one memory address in the majority of architectures).

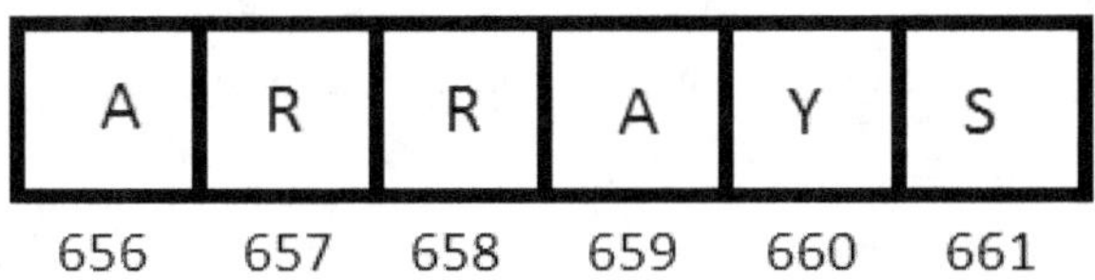

The elements are 'A', 'R', 'R', 'A', 'Y', and 'S', and the memory location is indicated by the number next to each. Each element is stored a single element apart since each character requires a single byte.

☐ Take another five-element array of integers with a storage requirement of four bytes per element.

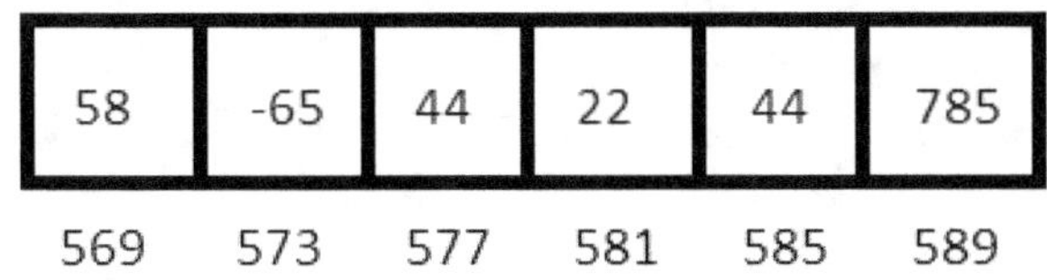

Each element in this case is separated by four bytes, or four memory locations.

- Using the following code snippet, we can determine the addresses of each element. –

int arr[n],i; //n is the size of array

for(i=0;i<n;i++)

printf("%d\t",&arr[i]);

2D array

A collection of homogenous components arranged in m rows and n columns make up a 2-dimensional array. The array elements are stored progressively in memory since the actual memory is sequential, as seen in the image below.

```
int arr[4][4]={
{56, 85, 82, 66},
{20, 56, 125, 785},
{96, 75, 21, 5},
{785, 45, 223, 451},
};
```

0th Row				1st Row				2nd Row				3rd Row			
56	85	82	66	20	56	125	785	96	75	21	5	785	45	223	451
600	604	608	612	616	620	624	628	632	636	640	644	648	652	656	660

- The integer array required four bytes of storage for each element. Each memory location is therefore four units apart from the others.
- The aforementioned storing technique is known as row-major order. The values are kept in this case row-by-row, starting with all of the items in the zeroth row and continuing with the first row and so forth.
- Base address + (i*n) + j //m X n matrix yields the address of the (i,j)th cell.
- Elements are kept column by column in a manner similar to column major order.
- Row-major order is used in the C programming language.

Multi-dimensional array

☐ More than two dimensions make for a multi-dimensional array.

☐ A three by m by n array is an example. It consists primarily of three two-dimensional arrays.

☐ As a result, to save it, the first two-dimensional array is stored first, then the second, and finally the third.

Chapter 37: SPARSE MATRICES

Sparse matrices:

- A sparse matrix is one in which the majority of the array's entries are 0.
- The precise number of zeroes required for a matrix to be referred to as a sparse matrix is not defined.
- The matrices below can be regarded as sparse.

0	22	0	1	0	0	0	0	55
0	0	0	0	0	1	55	0	9
0	8	2	0	0	4	0	0	0
4	0	0	0	3	0	0	0	0
78	0	0	0	0	0	0	4	9
0	4	0	2	0	71	3	0	0

- A universal matrix can be used to represent a sparse matrix. However, since the majority of the elements are zero, we can utilise alternative representations that take up less space.
- The 3-tuple form is one such illustration.
- Each element is represented by three fields in the three tuple form. The row number is the first field, followed by the column number and the value. However, we are not required to store zeros in three-tuple form.
- The first three rows of the aforementioned matrix's three-tuple form are as follows:

```
int sparse[][]={ 0,1,22,
0,3,1,
0,8,55,
1,5,1,
1,6,55,
1,8,9,
2,1,8, // And so on
};
```

☐ Think of a n x m matrix. Assume that there are x non-zero elements. We require 3*x storage in 3-tuple form. So if the 3-tuple form saves space when 3*x n*m. If not, this approach is not very effective.

Stacks:

- With a few limitations, a stack is a linear data structure similar to an array.

- In a stack, elements can only be added or removed from the end. Stack TOP is the name of this end.

- Due to this characteristic, a stack is also known as a Last-In-First-Out (LIFO) list.

- The terms "PUSH operation" and "POP operation" describe how an element is added or removed.

- The following is a visual illustration of stack insertion and deletion operations.

				D
			F	F
		T	T	T
	U	U	U	U
A	A	A	A	A

D				
F	F			
T	T	T		
U	U	U	U	
A	A	A	A	A

PUSH OPERATION POP OPERATION

- Since insertion and deletion are performed at one end of the list, we don't need to traverse the full list for these operations. • A stack can be represented using an array or a linked list. Therefore, the stack allows for insertion and deletion in O(1) time, or in a fixed amount of time.

- "Stack underflow" refers to what happens if we attempt to remove an element from a stack that is empty.

- In a similar vein, "Stack overflow" refers to the act of adding an element to an already full stack.

- The size of a stack is theoretically limitless. However, there is a practical limit. The limit for array representation is the array size, but the limit for linked list representation is the amount of RAM that is available.

Application of Stack

- Polish and reverse-Polish notation can be created from arithmetic expressions using a stack.Each arithmetic operator in a computer language has a priority. This priority can be used to judge an expression. Nevertheless, evaluating an expression in a computer is challenging.
- Pre-fix notation, also known as Polish notation, and post-fix notation, sometimes known as reverse-Polish notation, are two ways that the Polish mathematician Jan Lukasiewicz proposed to describe an arithmetic expression. It is said that the universal arithmetic expressions are in in-fix form.
- Expressions are shown in pre-fix and post-fix notations with the operator following or preceding the operands, respectively. As a result, there is no need for parenthesis to indicate which part should be evaluated first.
- Consider the expression

a+b*c

This is to be evaluated as

(a+(b*c))

The pre-fix notation of it is

+a*bc

And post-fix notation is

abc*+

☐ Now, a stack can be used to evaluate the expressions.

☐ We scan the expression and insert each element one at a time into a stack to evaluate the pre-fix operation. When there are two operands, we pop the operator immediately below it and evaluate that portion with the operator. Next, the outcome is added to the stack. The procedure is repeated till the stack is not empty.

☐ In a manner similar to post-fix operation, we scan the expression and push each element one at a time into a stack. When we come across an operator, we pop it together with the two operands that are immediately below it and evaluate that section along with the operator. Next, the outcome is added to the stack. The procedure is repeated till the stack is not empty.

☐ For +a*bc, + is pushed first, then a, *, b, and finally c. We have the two operands b and c together when c is pushed. It is assessed using the operator *. Let D be the outcome. The stack's structure is +aD when D is pushed. As two operands, a and D are now evaluated as a pair with +. The procedure ends when plus is popped because the stack is now empty. The end result is given by a+D.

Chapter 39: QUEUE

Queue:

- Like a stack, a queue is a linear data structure. However, unlike a stack, here insertion and deletion take place at opposite ends.
- As a result of this characteristic, it is also known as a FIFO list.
- The ENQUEUE and DEQUEUE processes stand for insertion and deletion, respectively.
- The end of the queue where the element is inserted is referred to as the TAIL, whilst the other end is referred to as the HEAD. So, at first, head equals tail.

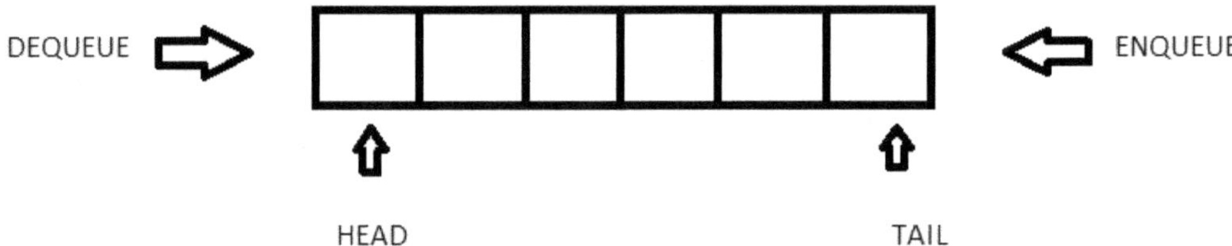

- An array or linked list can also be used to represent a queue.
- Queue underflow occurs when we DEQUEUE an empty queue. Queue overflow occurs when we ENQUEUE a full queue, similarly.
- When head=tail+1 in an array representation, the queue is full.

Circular queue

- A circular queue is one in which the following element is added at the first slot (provided it is free) after reaching the last position.
- In a typical queue, even though the beginning elements are empty (as a result of numerous dequeue processes), no more items can be added once the queue reaches its finish. The circular queue gets around this queue restriction.
- Both an array and a linked list can be used to express this.

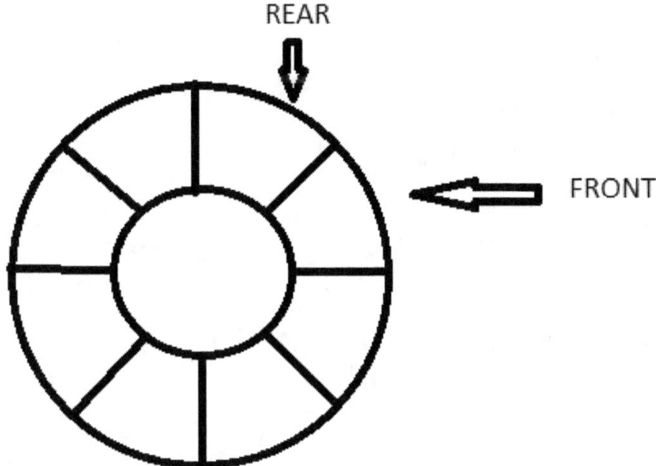

☐ When front=rear, the list in array representation is empty.

When front=0 and rear=n-1, where n is the array's size, or when rear=front-1, the list is full in array representation as well.

De-queue

- A double ended queue is the de-queue. At either end of the list, it permits insertion and deletion, but not in the middle.

- In essence, it is a generalisation of queue and stack.

REFERENCES

1. Fundamentals of computer by P K Sinha

2. Programming in C by Reema Thereja

3. Programming in ANSI C by E Balagurusamy

4. O'REILLY, "Practical C Programming", 3rd Edition

5. Yashavant P.kanetkar, "Let Us C", 5th Edition

6. Brian W. kernighan and Dennis M. Ritchie, "The C Programming Language"

7. Greg Perry, "C by Example"

8. Stephen Prata, "C Primer Plus", 5th Edition

Book Summary

The revolutionary manual "Computing Excellence: Empowering Future Engineers" evaluates the vital role that computing will take in determining the direction of engineering in the future. In this insightful book, readers travel through the fascinating confluence of innovation and technology, observing the significant impact it has on the profession of engineering.

The initial section of the book lays the foundation for understanding how gadgets has evolved into a vital tool for contemporary engineers. A comprehensive overview is given on the use of computational approaches, AI, and data analytics in simplifying every aspect of engineering, from design and modeling to problem-solving and optimization.

"Computing Excellence" illustrates the revolutionary possibilities of cutting-edge technologies like machine learning, IoT, and cloud computing in engineering applications through real-world case studies and industry insights. The need for encouraging digital literacy and a multidisciplinary approach to education are additionally highlighted, permitting the following generation of engineers to make full use of computing capabilities.

In the end, "Computing Excellence" creates an appealing image of a future where engineers equipped with computational skills lead the way in addressing difficult global concerns, from developing sustainable infrastructure to creating revolutionary goods. Anyone who is interested in the intersection of engineering and computing will find this book to be a priceless resource, delivering a glimpse into the exciting future possibilities.

UNESCO LAUREATE Prof. Sir Bashiru Aremu
Professor & Vice Chancellor
@ Crown University Int'l Chartered Inc. (CUICI) USA

Prof. Dr. K. Mahammad Rafi
Founder President @ eSkillGrow Virtual University LLC, USA
Board Member & Global Director
@ Crown University Int'l Chartered Inc. (CUICI) USA

Dr. Mir Iqbal Faheem
Professor & Director of Technical Campus,
Deccan Group of Institutions, Hyderabad, India

Dr. Mohd Minhajuddin Aquil
Associate Professor, Department of Civil Engineering,
Deccan College of Engineering and Technology,
Hyderabad, India

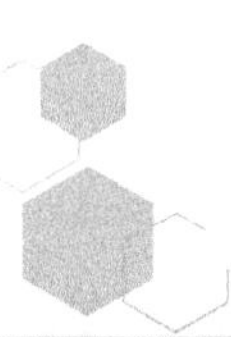

Registered in "Global Register of Publishers"